"Kerry Hope's story highlights a real sense of vulnerability and authenticity. It's refreshing and empowering to me as a woman in my forties to read something so raw and full of truth. Bravo, brave woman."

Melissa Herzog,
House of AUM and *Wild & Awake Circle Training Creatrix*

"Kerry Hope, you are an inspiration. You have written a guide for the healing journey, honoring personal truth, choosing self-love, and modeling empowerment for all women."

Jasmine Astra-elle Grace,
Founder of Jyoti Veda – Light, Wisdom, Wellness

"A beautiful weaving of ancient wisdom teachings and modern storytelling. Kerry Hope authentically shares her journey to self while teaching us bravery and the importance of finding your own truth."

Erica Fullen,
Intuitive Healer and Meditation Teacher

"A compelling journey of heart and bravery with a reverent nod to the seasons of womanhood."

Jen Waine,
Astrologer and Moon Maven Creatrix

"Kerry Hope is a spark of light in a chaotic world. Her courageous choice to live an authentic life should be inspiring to us all."

Dawn Thompson,
Dawn of the New Era

"Kerry Hope shares her journey in such a powerful way in this book. Her story is a demonstration of love in action, and witnessing her self-love as she steps into her authenticity has been a gift. I hope that in reading this book you are inspired to dive into your own heart and bring forth your light to shine for others."

Sarah Beth Adel,
Owner and Creatrix of *Sacred Rose Medicinals*

YOUR TRIPLE GODDESS

A PATH TO SELF-LOVE, EMPOWERMENT, AND HEALING

KERRY HOPE

Published by the Compassionate Mind Collaborative.

 CMC

Edited by Heather Doyle Fraser

Cover design by Dino Marino, dinomarino.com

Interior layout and design by Dino Marino

Proofed by Julie Homon

Paperback ISBN: 978-1-7372006-5-9

eBook ISBN: 978-1-7372006-6-6

*For my father, Steve, who succumbed to cancer
as the Seasons transitioned from Winter to Spring in 2009.*

I heard your message.

All In Due Time

*The Autumn leaves feel heavy from the saturation of cool droplets.
All in due time, the leaves dry and fly through the sky on the winds
of change.*

*The Winter grasses are stiff with the heavy blanket of frozen dew
wrapped around each blade.*
All in due time, the warmth of the bright sun melts it away.

*The Spring buds of the trees feel soaked and sorrowful.
All in due time, the birds sip and pause from their song to quench
their thirst.*

*The Summer Earth releases the warmth of the rugged terrain
only to succumb to the brush of coolness across the horizon,
All in due time, bare feet release love in each step taken forward.*

TABLE OF CONTENTS

INTRODUCTION

To sort out the details of how and why I have arrived at this place in my life, it's essential for me to reflect upon the significant moments and experiences in my life path up to this point. This reflection has been crucial as my life has unfolded during this transformational Season.

When people observe where I was and where I am now, I can hear their questions in my mind: How did you get here? How did you decide to change the course and direction of your life completely? To all the eyes that witnessed my everyday existence, the overall review would have been this:

"Kerry is a happy, go-getting mother of two healthy and loving children. She has a successful career, and is a business creator. She has a great relationship with her mother, beautiful and meaningful relationships with friends, and a husband that is an awesome guy. They have a wonderful marriage and relationship."

All of those attributes of my life were true! And yet, there were hidden emotions and kept secrets that stayed safe behind the smiles. There were kicks under the table and puppet strings that held up the marionette doll so perfectly that no one would suspect a false existence. There is always more than what we see on the surface. Even my eyes couldn't see what was happening behind the scenes. Time reveals the truth, though, and I was the pioneer of this new terrain. I had to examine my life as I knew it first, honestly, and once the discovery of Self was initiated, there was no going back.

The unfolding of my life transformation appeared to happen quickly and spontaneously. The truth is that this transformation occurred methodically through the seeking of truth over time. I look back at all the details, the moments, and the rememberings of my life, and I realize I have always been a seeker of truth. My life path would shake outside of all the norms. As I continue to allow and watch my own life story unfold, I hope that it will enable others to pay attention to the details of their own lives and find Self-love. Love of thy Self is an ultimate achievement. It all comes back to love.

I believe that we all come into our lives with lessons and learnings that will help us evolve into more open-hearted, open-minded humans. These lessons will be different for every single person. I believe these lessons will continue to show up until we can understand and learn from them, accomplish our goals, or embrace and heal the wounds that hold us in a stagnant place. We get frustrated with our loved ones when they are not "learning" what they need to learn. Similarly, family and friends in our circles may have to witness us go through our own often painful lessons.

In this theory, I remind myself that my lessons are my own. I do not want to project my experience or learnings onto others. In turn, the people I love with all my heart are going through their own experiences in life that I cannot control. All we can do in our human life is stand as a witness to their path, their journey, their own experiences, and their lessons. Even when you witness your loved ones going through chaotic and messy life experiences, the real challenge is to love them anyway. I believe as humans, we are capable of supporting our partners, children, friends, and family members through challenging times. While witnessing, we can also find grace, compassion, and unconditional love for them. That is genuinely elevated living.

One of my greatest teachers and most prominent witnesses in this life is my father. I lost his earthly presence to cancer as the seasons transitioned from Winer to Spring in 2009. He worked so hard to keep his frail body well enough to board a plane from Florida to frigid Ohio in February so that he could meet his first grandson. I was in complete denial that my father only had weeks to live. I was also in the clutches of postpartum and the myriad emotions that all new mothers experience. Still, watching my father nap with my newborn baby on his chest was my most significant memory from that time.

My father, Steve, was one of those unforgettable guys. He brought so much enthusiasm to his life daily. He lit up the room with his sense of humor and laughter. My father was my person. After his transition, I truly understood the magnificence of our relationship. I have grown so spiritually connected to my father for the past decade, and communication with him has been comical and easeful. Flickering lights when I needed answers or hearing – right at the perfect time – the Stevie Wonder song we danced to at my wedding are just a couple of the significant ways he reached out to me. He was with me throughout my year of life transition and is still with me every day.

During my year of Seasons, I was on the phone with my father's widow, my stepmother, Lesa, in a moment of despair. She was holding space for me to process through the hurt and pain at a time of grief and loss. And in the perfect moment, she paused and said to me, "Did your Dad ever tell you about the boat he wanted to buy before he died?" Through sniffly tears and a little confusion, I responded, "No? I didn't even know he was looking at boats." She continued to explain all the details of the boat and where they were going to dock it, and then she continued to say, "Yeah, he already had a name picked out for the boat too: *All In Due Time*."

Once again, my father found a way to communicate with me. This all will pass. You will get to the other side of this transition, this divorce, these pains of grief . . . All In Due Time.

My name is Kerry Hope. Thank you for allowing me this time and space to be with you, for you to hold my words and my story for me.

Giving grace is a practice that I work on daily. As you join me as a witness to my story and the unfolding of all my lessons, I hope you can use this experience to practice standing as a witness to me. Even if you do not know or love me, just pretend as if you do! Witness me in my story. And who knows? Maybe your righteous act of non-judgment will bring you the same experience in your life. We are all here as humans doing the best we can. Welcome to these pages of my experience as a human.

I hope that this story may lead you back to your own heart. May the story of my life transformation inspire you to honor your own story, journey, and truth. I am honored to share what I have learned, backed by courage, guided wisdom, and the practical ways and practices I found to get me through this lifestyle overhaul. Finally, may you find love and grace as you journey with me through my story. We have one precious life to live, and may we all find our way in this journey through love.

PROLOGUE

PATH OF THE JOURNEY

As a young adult, I loved perusing bookstores. The Barnes & Noble chain of stores was significant because I often studied in the store's cafe when I was in college. I always had a hot chai tea in hand even before it became a trendy, expensive drink. I would allow myself study breaks and walk around and explore all the different sections and book categories. I remember finding books in each area, TRAVEL, ARTS, FICTION & SELF IMPROVEMENT, and in some cases, a book would literally fall off the shelf to grab my attention.

These days, I peruse Instagram just as I used to peruse the bookstore all of those years ago. I discover book recommendations from social accounts I follow or book covers promoted through catchy images from publishing companies. So I was completely surprised when a dear friend of mine shared her experience on her most recent trip to Barnes & Noble. She said, "Do you know that there is now a LIFE TRANSFORMATION section at the bookstore?" At that moment, I felt an array of emotions. First off, with a feeling of dread. *So many people are writing about life transformation. Is there space for another book?* Then to relief. *If there is a whole section in a national book store on Life Transformation, then there are people interested in and hungry to learn more about how to transform their lives.* I knew at this moment that I had to continue my book-writing journey.

I didn't want to tell my personal story, but I wanted to create a map of how I made it through my transformation, hoping that it might help you too. Each major part coincides with the seasons of the year and the seasons of my life. They provide the framework for my story and every story of endings and new beginnings.

In my early adulthood, I began a spiritual journey to find ways to connect with nature and to find answers to the big question of *why are we even here on planet Earth*? If you are in tune with the newer age thinking, which technically is not new, you will undoubtedly encounter the chakra (chak·ra) energy theories. Learning through this wisdom dates back from 1500 to 500BC in India, and I, too, discovered I could relate to these concepts and understand the principles around the chakra system. With this system, I learned a language in which I could speak, "energy."

In my story, I use this language to communicate the lessons I learned and the support I was able to give and receive from my archetypes of Maiden, Mother, and Crone. The discovery of the "energy" language lead me to the wisdom that we are all connected as one giant energy system. Therefore, I also learned to listen to the language that nature speaks. When I began to listen truly, I grew and strengthened my heart and Soul.

The Seasons of the Year: Winter, Spring, Summer, Fall

For our journey together, I am honored to share the vulnerable details of my life transformation and my lessons through the lens and framework of the Seasons. Hopefully, every human on Earth may have some connection and reference to the Four Seasons of the year, but I hope that all humans will continue to find ways to see how our lives are synced in coordination with Earth. How can we truly live within the Four Seasons of the year to optimize our health and lives?

Since the year's Four Seasons are cyclical and continuous, there is no beginning or end. Each Season offers lessons on how we can mirror the same patterns and energy that our great Mother Earth demonstrates to us. Seasons of sowing and planting to harvesting abundance, to laying dormant. As creatures of our planet, we can find ways to incorporate the same patterns and processes. We continue to move in and out of each Season.

I chose to begin in Autumn for my journey, as this was when the most significant part of my journey started. However, you will learn that other moments in previous seasons lead up to these crucial moments. Although my shared journey ended in Summer, my evolution will always continue. The essence of each Season in which we will journey through my story will be the same for all the years of life still to come.

The Seasons of Our Lives: Maiden, Mother, Crone

I have also learned to embody the teachings of the Seasons of Our Lives in my life path. The Seasons of Our Lives are the four main archetypes that we live through in each stage of life: the Inner Child, the Maiden, the Mother, and the Crone. For women, we start as a young child from birth to our teen years and are often referred to as our Inner Child. The Inner Child is the persona that we bring into our lives. Some say it's our most authentic form of ourselves, as the Soul or Ego has not yet been conditioned by family or society. Therefore, we are of our most authentic Selves in this Season of Life. Our innocence also helps us shape our viewpoints and is incredibly impressionable to our upbringing. The Inner Child is an embodiment that will carry through in all other stages of our lives. (In this year of Seasons in my life, I spent most of my time connecting to the Triple Goddess of Maiden, Mother, and Crone, although you will find a letter to my Inner Child and some play from her thrown in on the journey.)

After exiting childhood, we develop into our Maiden, transitioning from our teen years through to young adults. The Season of the Maiden is seen as the prime years of a woman's life experience; this mindset stems from the Patriarchal systems in our society. Conversely, if you ask a woman beyond her fortieth or fiftieth year of life, she would likely say her prime would be entering or living through her Crone stage of life. The Crone signifies a time when you have gained the knowledge and wisdom that gives you a sense of freedom, Self-Love, and disregard for others' opinions.

The Maiden learns to embrace her sensuality and sexuality, feels into the longing and desires of her body, and also learns the power of this commodity. The Maiden continues to gain wisdom and grow physically and emotionally. In addition, she is subject to personal and environmental conditioning, mainly from her culture, society, family, friends, and of course, media. These are incredibly impressionable years of a woman's life and a Season that can be full of life's incredible lessons. The Maiden represents fertility and growth.

After leaving maidenhood, the young woman then transitions into the Mother. Regardless of whether women conceive and give birth to a baby, all women journey through the Season of the Mother. We embrace this time of our lives when we adopt and become Mothers to a pet, birth a new career, or become a nurturer in our community. During the Season of the

Mother, we learn to give all of ourselves to something outside of us. For many, our value depends on how well we "Mother" the people in our lives, our jobs, co-workers, or small groups within our society. These can be the most rewarding years of our lives, and when the Mother can lose herself to fill her role in society. The Mother truly represents love and protection.

The Mother will eventually transition into the Crone, the final Season of Life for a woman. This is when all the knowledge we have gained through childhood, the Maiden Season, and throughout the Mother Season crystallize into pure wisdom. It is the Season of Life we could all strive to reach; it's the final stage of life's journey well lived. The Crone represents wisdom.

Regardless of how old we are or where we are in our life paths, irrespective of our Season of Life, we as spiritual human beings can learn from all Four of our Seasons of Life at any given time. We can access our Inner Child, our Maidens, our Mother, and our Crone energy within our Selves. For Men, all the Seasons that would link to the significance of Maiden/Mother/Crone are categorized as Hunter/Father/Sage. All men can learn from their wisdom as Inner Child, the Hunter, the Father, and the Sage. These archetypes represent truth, growth, love, and wisdom.

Our lives can be enriched when we tap into our inner wisdom from each archetype of Maiden/Mother/Crone or Hunter/Father/Sage. In my journey through my life transformation, I asked, "What would my Maiden say to me now?" or "How would the archetype of Mother support me?" In reference to my Crone in this book, it is my older, wiser Self that I am referencing, not an actual older woman such as a Grandmother. I tap into the energy and lessons from each of my archetypes and weave their wisdom in to help me tell my story.

In times of distress during my journey, I leaned heavily on these archetypes to help me through the complex and strenuous parts of the path. In each Season of Life, you will notice that I call on the Triple Goddess of my Maiden, Mother, and Crone for assistance. I write them letters and have conversations and dialogue with them as if they were right here with me on every step of this journey (because they were).

Eight Chakra Energy Fields: Root, Sacral, Solar Plexus, Heart, Throat, Third Eye, Crown Chakras

Finally, what helped me through this journey to the other side of my life transition was the embodiment of the chakra (chak·ra) energy fields.. Our bodies are all designed with the same and or very similar anatomy as humans.

Regardless of whether a person identifies as a man, woman, or transgender, we all have and carry energy fields in our bodies. These energy fields are a form of communication throughout our bodies and from the body to the mind.

There are many beautiful sources and ways to learn about the chakra energy fields associated with the human body. The psychological studies of the chakras originated from ancient Hinduism and Tantric Buddhism practices. There are seven chakra energy wheels related to seven areas, nerves, or organs that can affect or support the energy in our bodies. The main idea around Chakra energy is to have unblocked and open energy to thrive in a healthy, human existence.

Each component correlates beautifully to my body's chakra energetic field throughout this life transition. My chakra energy was also in sync with the Seasons. Therefore, we can give attention to our Body, Mind, and Spirit throughout our daily lives. Here are brief descriptions of each of the seven chakras and how I utilized the energy around each of them on my path through transformation.

The Root Chakra is where we feel our security and safety. This energy is felt at the base of your spine, tailbone, and perineum. When I honor my Root Chakra energy, I work to ground myself, feel stable, and manage my sense of security.

The Sacral Chakra energy can be honored in the lower abdomen or below the navel. This energy supports creativity, sexuality, and ways to incorporate new opportunities. I actively enjoy pleasure, play, and sensual enjoyment when I honor my Sacral Chakra energy.

The Solar Plexus Chakra is located in the upper abdomen and stomach area. This energy, when activated, creates power and confidence and allows a sense of control in our own lives.

The Heart Chakra energy resides in the chest and hearts of our bodies. This energy is where we feel and express our love. When we embody and feel into our Heart Chakra energy, we can learn so much about how to love and how we can be loved.

The Throat Chakra wheel of energy is located in your throat. When embodied, it represents our ability to communicate. When we embrace the power around the Throat Chakra, we learn to express our values, desires, needs, and truths.

The Third Eye Chakra energy is located in between our eyebrows and forehead. When healthy, we embrace more intuition, inner knowing, and wisdom. Here, we can foster our thoughts and discernment and our abilities to make decisions.

The Crown Chakra energy is the final energy source associated with our body, located at the very top of our heads or crowns of our heads. This is the energy that allows for our spiritual connection to great sources. For example, when we embody our Crown Chakra energy, we can experience a great connection to nature and our surroundings.

As you journey alongside me, my intention is for you to embody the lessons around the seasons of the year, the Seasons of Life, and awareness around your chakra energy, just as I have. Throughout each Season, you will see how the dialogue with my inner Maiden, Mother, and Crone can model how simple and easy it can be to create a conversation with your inner Triple Goddess. In addition, you will find a visualization practice to connect with your Maiden, Mother, and Crone at the end of each Season. Finally, the last section provides helpful resources, rituals, and anchors for each Season as you journey on your path to transformation.

I

THE SEASON OF AUTUMN

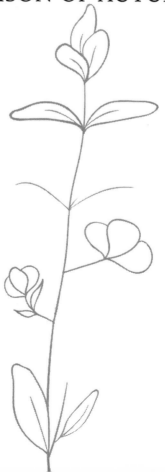

HONORING YOUR HEART'S LONGING

We gather all we have sowed with arms full of abundance and gratitude.

This is the Season to take stock of your life: examine all the jars filled with the fruit of your Summer efforts. Did you work your landscape of life to fulfill all that you need? Are there any areas you need to supplement to secure your happiness for the Autumn Season?

What is your Soul longing for in this Autumn Season?

Rest and reflection allow you to see the joys you obtained in the Summer. Now is the time to create comfort and warmth in our homes and hearts. Allow yourself to fall into the sofa or your bed with a sense of peace and coziness. Find quiet moments to notice all you have in your home or space that brings fulfillment.

How can you fill up your cupboards in your heart's chambers? Do you feel your heart full of love and contentment as you slowly allow each breath to exhale a little bit longer in these shorter days? Our hearts can genuinely hold so much.

The golden yellows, dark reds, and brilliant oranges surround us now as we bask in the final days of the warmth of the sun.

Our breaths can be lengthened one at a time, inhaling the smell of transitions in the air, exhaling all the knowledge we have gained.

How can you allow yourself to transition with the turning of the leaves? Can you take a moment to identify a tree near you on your commute to work? Can you see the brilliant color of her leaves as if they are wrapped around you? Allow yourself to change with the tree in this transition process. Feel in your core what it might be like to release your leaves each year as a tree.

What will you leave behind as you enter the Season of dying and release?

This is Autumn, dear one.

Gather all that serves you now. Release all that doesn't suit you.

Letter to the Mother, October 2019

Dear Mother,

I hope this letter finds you well, and I believe you are in your final phase of completing your Autumn Equinox creative work and projects. I miss you, and I miss our daily chats and texts. The truth is, Mother, I have no idea who else I can turn to right now. You see, I have been diving into women's empowerment training with this incredible group of women. We are all asking more considerable, more profound questions to help us better understand what our Soul's path entails. We want to explore how to live a true purpose-filled, authentic life so that we may be able to help other women do the same in their own lives.

This study has been truly eye-opening and heart-expanding for me. The lessons created all resonate with me and what I genuinely want to share with others. However, in my discovery of Self, I find that I feel incomplete even as I pour my heart's longing out through journal writing and creating dialogue in our group.

You know me, Mother, and you understand that I have always been a seeker. A seeker to find more meaningful and conscious ways of living. I wake up and look around at my day-to-day life and wonder what else there is still for me to discover. I feel incomplete and notice that I have this amazing life with a great, loving husband and a father to our two exceptional, healthy children. We live in this beautiful home in a safe, rural community. I have a great career accompanied by passion projects. I am supported and loved by friends and family, travel and vacations, and care for myself in many beautiful ways. So how can I still feel unfulfilled?

I feel as if I am longing for something different. I feel as if I am not in the best space to grow and flourish into the woman I want to become, the mother I am told to be, and the lover I am meant to be. There it is! That is my little secret. I just don't feel like I am in the right relationship anymore. Even as I write this down, I don't know what that means. I have committed to being married forever and ever, so is that what I am supposed to do?

Mother, please share your wisdom with me. I need help sorting out my feelings around this longing for something new. I know that people can go through a midlife crisis, but I don't know what that means either. I know that I am uncertain and scared, and I don't know who to turn to anymore.

Welcoming your wisdom and advice,

Kerry Hope

Throat Chakra: Lessons on Using My Voice

My Maiden whispers to Me: *"Hey. You know you can speak up, right? Why are you acting so shy and embarrassed about what you want? Can you just speak up for both of us already? I might not have been brave enough to be fully honest about my deepest desires and thoughts in my prime Maiden years, but look at you in this life now! You can do this Kerry Hope. You can speak up on what you truly want in your life."*

Me: *"I know, I know. I remember how it felt to feel confused and how much easier it was for me to dismiss those thoughts when I was younger. I was just trying to stay the course in my life, and remember, it was massively taboo back then, thank God times have changed."*

My Maiden: *"Do you know that tightness in your throat that you feel when you are emotional and feeling vulnerable with others? It's me, getting your attention, and wanting you to use the confidence that you have now to SPEAK UP!"*

Me: *"Oh, that's been you this whole time?"*

My Maiden: *"Yep! The energy around your throat has been blocked for years, lady. This is because you have suppressed so many thoughts and emotions for a long, long time."*

Me: *"Okay, okay, I know. I can't help but want to make everyone feel comfortable and at ease around me. I don't like when people get upset with me, and I have always had a hard time articulating my feelings or arguing points without getting emotional. And you know this all too well, Missy. I recall as a teenager you would just run off from arguments and get angry. Remember those moments?"*

My Maiden: *"I sure do, and damn I hated how I behaved, and I look back with regret. However, I also wish I was better at sharing my feelings without feeling judged. I wish that I would have had more courage instead of deflecting my curiosity."*

Me: *"And look at me now, I think I'm doing pretty darn good for myself!"*

My Maiden: *"Umm, Kerry, I love you, but no. You are NOT okay. You are trying to live out a life and lifestyle that you are not okay with anymore. So yeah, I am tugging at your throat and making it hard for you to swallow. Why? Well, because you are in the best place of your life to make some changes. To realign to your truer and more authentic, beautiful Self.*

Come on, Kerry Hope. Let's do this. You've got me, your adventurous and free-spirited Maiden Self, who is dying to experience more than what is going on in your current Mother stage of life. Sorry, not to knock your choices, but come on! Let's get brave and speak up!"

Me: *"Yeah, Yeeeah, I got it. Okay. (deep breath). Ugh. This is going to be so hard. How do I even start?"*

My Maiden: *"Keep breathing. You have everything you need right now to be brave. I will keep reminding you that I am here with you. I want you to feel back into the energy you once carried in your Maiden years of life. Who do you know right now that will be able to listen to your deepest desires and longings? Start there, you've got this, Kerry Hope."*

STREAMS OF LONGING FOR SOMETHING DIFFERENT

It was a beautiful Autumn day on the grounds of Sacred GEO, which is the name for what many call the open grass and wetlands that sit alongside my home. I expected a group of women to come, as they did each month, and join me in a women's circle to discuss the theme of The Wild Women Project for the New Moon in Scorpio. As a circle leader for the The Wild Women Project for the past three years, this was always a highlight of my month. I longed to be the space-holder for women to come together, share their lives, set intentions for the coming month, and be witnessed and heard. Each gathering around the new moon had a different theme to discuss. At this particular time, I presented the ideas of *Streams of Longing* and what *desires* we could honor for our lives in this phase of the moon.

As I sat on the front porch, ready to greet my guests, my phone continuously pinged with text notifications. Messages of regrets for not being able to attend, and other sentiments of "So sorry, something suddenly came up!" Feeling a little disappointed, I sat in my rocker. I closed my eyes and took a deep, long breath. "The right people show up at the right time. The right people show up at the right time." I repeated this mantra silently to myself over and over. I knew that no matter who came to this circle, it would still be precisely right.

The next moment, a car comes rolling up the driveway. I see two shiny, smiley, happy faces that I know and love. I smiled so hard while doing a little energetic dance, which I always do when seeing my friends. It had only been a short few weeks since I spent a long weekend with these two friends in August at the Wild Women Fest in upstate New York. These two women are strong and open-hearted and have brought such wisdom to me. So this moment felt exactly right.

We grabbed our journals and a tea and walked down to the teepee structure that sits in the corner by the property's wetlands. This teepee structure has held so many incredible moments in my last five years. Moments in this space include meditation circles, emotional release ceremonies, and beautiful tea ceremonies. This structure held many deep conversations with family and friends and even an impromptu late-night karaoke session to Tiny Turner with a group of wild women. As I sit in this same structure that has held so many precious memories with these two beautiful friends of mine, I felt seen and heard. In this sweet coziness of the teepee, I felt a small whisper start to come out from me. It was here that I began to acknowledge my truth and true longing and found enough bravery to share what was in my heart.

We listened to each other speak with full attentiveness as we sat knee to knee. One woman shared how she was longing for more validation in her workplace. The challenges and discrepancies of being a woman in corporate America were heavy on her heart. She continued to say how she longs for more leadership opportunities within the organization to grow her career. My other friend spoke about her hope for more freedoms in her everyday life with work and the societal constructs around her relationships. She was longing for a healthy relationship that might be outside the norms of our culture's view of one man and one woman. We each took a turn to speak and to be heard by each other as women do in a circle ceremony. We were open, honest, and vulnerable.

(As a typical rule of women's circles, we never share the words or experiences of our Sister outside of the sacred circle. For the sake of explanation and to help provide the context of my experiences, permission was granted to share the basic ideas shared by the others.)

It was my turn to share. "How can the ritual of this circle help me uncover a deeply held longing or desire?" I knew I was in good hands and in a safe space when the words rolled out of my mouth. "I am longing for something different," I said. Oh shit. There it was, like a big pile of bouncy red jello sitting on the floor, and all three of us just stopped and stared at it. I immediately wanted to shove those words back into my mouth.

What did I even mean by that? I pretended to ask myself like I wasn't sure. I continued to explain how my life is perfect in so many ways, but I still felt like I desired something different. The women tightly held their gaze with me. I felt like every word coming out of my mouth was just a test to see what it felt and sounded like. I knew that these two women were the barometer of bullshit and knowing. They nodded their heads and heard all my words. I knew at this moment that there was no going back to the moment of not acknowledging my inner desires. I knew that this was the initiation into something bigger than I could not even imagine. I knew that if I kept this longing and desire in the dark space of my Soul's heart that I would eventually crumble.

I knew I truly desired to be with a woman instead of the man I had chosen to marry 17 years prior. I had no idea what this moment would mean for me at the time. At this moment, I was sure that everything was still going to be okay, no matter how the future unfolded. However much denial I granted myself in this Season, things would eventually become difficult and complicated. I was sitting in a place of comfort and did not know what the discomfort would feel like on the other side. However, there was enough longing within me to tiptoe into the unknown to find out.

Third Eye Chakra: Lessons On Intuitive Knowing

My Crone whispers to Me: *"Well hello, sweetheart, what a fun surprise to have your attention!"*

Me: *"Oh, hello my dear ol' Soul. Are you doing well these days?"*

My Crone: *"Well, as a matter of fact, I am doing just fine, better than fine. I am elated that you are finally paying attention to yourself and taking more moments to listen. Sweet Kerry Hope, you have given so much and continue to give so much, and now I see that you are taking more care of yourself. I know it feels very odd at first, and you are struggling with feeling selfish and guilty for taking time away from the kids to do a little self-discovery work, but don't you dare let ANYONE make you feel bad for doing what you need to do in order to create a more awakened life, this time will make you a greater Mother, just wait and see."*

Me: *"I hear you dear one, and I am trying not to let the opinions of others affect me, but they just do. I have always cared too much about what other people think of me."*

My Crone: (chuckling) *"Oh I know sweetheart, I have watched you struggle with that for many years, poor thing. However, I am here to remind you that you will get through that phase soon enough. Trust me. In time, you will build up your inner knowing strength to trust yourself. You will soon find the strength to weather the hard conversations in order to thrive as your best Self in all of your relationships. And the best part that is yet to come . . . You are going to stop caring about what other people think of you. Not because you are a hard and uncaring person, but because you will learn in time that it is most important to stop taking everything so personally, this will Free your Soul! You will have the wisdom to know how to fully support your emotional needs without needing validation or approval."*

Me: *"This all sounds so dreamy and amazing dear Crone, but I just don't know how I am going to overcome my current issues of worthiness and self-confidence. I feel like your description of my Future Self is truly unobtainable."*

My Crone: *"Nothing that your heart desires is unobtainable. You are the creator of your own story. You are the map maker for your life path and journey. How you choose to see yourself is going to grant the permission of others to see you in that the same way."*

Me: *"Okay, this future me sounds amazing. So how do I get to that place in my life, my wise one?"*

My Crone: *"You listen to yourself. You pay attention to your intuition. You live and breathe each moment of your day-to-day in clarity and being fully present. You've got this, Kerry Hope. Oh, and don't forget, you have amazing women at your back to support your growth."*

CONTAINER OF WOMEN FOR SUPPORT

"Behind every great man, there is a great woman."

When I hear this phrase, it feels endearing and true to what I know from witnessing countless couples personally and the iconic partnerships we may all know. (One of my favorites would be Michelle and Barack.) However, I always heard this little voice in my mind say it differently. "Behind every great woman was a group of other strong women." This phrase also rings true to my heart and has proven accurate throughout my life.

I love to share and promote the campaign of women supporting other women. I often provide examples of how beneficial it is to support and help other women. For many of us, we thrive in our endeavors when we feel supported. Listening to The goop Podcast with Gwyneth Paltrow while driving home from work one day, I learned that women overall have better health conditions when they regularly surround themselves with their friends. I was not surprised by this report. The amount of laughter and joy my girlfriends have brought me over my adult years has been Soul-lifting.

When I interact with women – my best friends or others I may only see through yoga or women's circles – I feel a difference in my overall well-being. Feeling supported and loved by other women is a sensation I require daily for a healthy life. If I have the love and support from my female friends, knowing that they genuinely have my best interest at heart, I feel at my optimal health.

The Spring before this Season of Autumn, I was overjoyed to join in a hybrid yoga, mindfulness, and meditation teacher training that incorporated a new study of our cycles and Seasons of Life through the Wheel of the Year. It was an invitation to learn through my dear friend many of the lessons, daily living habits, and rituals that she had learned from her mentor and teacher. This training was perfect, and I was yearning for it. The additional learning, growth, and wisdom were precisely what I was looking for. This training represented a call I felt to share more with other women and empower them in their own lives, just as I was empowering myself. I read the initial description of the training and the words came flying out of my mouth while I was sipping coffee and reading through my emails, "FUCK, YES!" This is Wild & Awake, and this is for me.

I quickly grabbed my overly obligated calendar and began flipping through month by month through the end of Spring of 2020. Each weekend designated for this training program was completely open on my calendar. I was meant to be in this training. I knew that this container of women would be able to hold me through a massive life-changing experience that was coming from my inner knowing. My intuition said this is it! Saying yes to this training allowed me to feel supported and loved by a group of women who would witness my life's greatness unfold.

AN ODE TO WOMEN

To the women in my life, who I hold ever so close to my heart,

My Soul filled up with so much joy when meeting each of you at the start.

To the Sisters who heard my cries during the dark night

Then wrapped me up in blankets of love and light.

ALL the women who love so fiercely; you can feel it through your bones.

Allowing love and laughter; true nourishment for their homes.

The Sisters who remember to live within nature, creating memories in a beautiful way,

Initiating the sounds of cackles, moans, and howls come what may.

To my best friend and I, who swapped blood at fingertips with a pact,

That no matter the bruises and burdens, we will never return back.

To all the Maidens, Mothers, and Crones in my life who can see me at every stage,

We witness our own gifts and purpose while creating a legacy on every page.

Thank you to the women who hold up the mirrors framed in silver and gold,

Showing and teaching me so many lessons as my own journey unfolds.

We circle knee to knee, listen and hold the space for each other's visions,

Navigating together in council to support each other and our own decisions.

Tears rest on my cheeks with so much gratitude for this beautiful band

of friends. My heart – so happy, so full – with connections to the Sisterhood that will stand a lifetime.

ACCEPTANCE OF ATTRACTION

The nerves and excitement that filled my friend's home were palpable as the ten women gathered together for the first time to embark on the wildest, spiritual ride together. The Wild & Awake Full Circle Goddess Training was initiated in July of 2019. We committed to a weekend each month for a ten month journey to learn techniques to empower ourselves and strengthen our self-worth. Once the training is complete, we would then set out to demonstrate, empower, and teach other women to strengthen their own self-worth through Body, Mind, and Spirit.

Within the first few months together, we learned about: how to live within the Seasons of the year; astrology archetypes and energies around the moon phases; ways to incorporate a healthy diet, body movement, the importance of rest, and care for our bodies. We discussed ways to cultivate a connection to Self, Nature, and our relationships. We were doing the work, as the phrase goes. *Doing the work* is the term used in spiritual communities to describe the process of learning about your inner Self through healing the pains, traumas, and wounds endured over a lifetime. This group of women showed up together to be vulnerable and honest with themselves. The first gathering of this group of Wild & Awake women was where I first met – Her – the incredible woman who would completely change the trajectory of my life.

Within the first few moments of meeting Kristen, I had a sensation of curiosity and a weird desire to impress her and gain her attention. I sat next to her in the circle and could feel her energy solid and guarded. This woman had inked tattoos on her arms, shoulders, and her feet, and I was distracted by the sensation of wanting to touch her soft skin. She kept her gaze forward, and the energy around her heart seemed blocked. Why was she here, and how did she get here? I was so curious. As we all took turns introducing ourselves and answering such questions, I was intrigued by every word that came out of her mouth. Her mouth, her lips. I found myself staring at her for longer than what seemed to be a normal amount of time. I couldn't help but feel all this curiosity and wonder. *A lesbian woman.* I quickly concluded. Huh, here in this very Wild & Awake training? I wonder if she has a partner, significant other, a girlfriend? I continued to analyze.

The weekend continued, and as we participated in different sessions: yoga and body movement, contemplation and journaling, group shares, and even during the meals, I noticed how nervous I felt around this woman, Kristen. During this training, I was with three of my closest girlfriends and felt like they saw curiosity all over my face. I was trying to hide it. I stayed focused on the teachings, the content, and the curriculum. I stayed focused on my primary intention to be in this training and present in the moment. Over the next few months of training, there were several little moments that I knew were significant. I knew that she was noticing my attention and the energy between us when we were lying next to each other in the final yoga posture of savasana. Our arms would innocently brush against each other while in the kitchen preparing tea for our afternoon sessions. There was this nervous excitement when we arrived for our weekend training each month, and we both felt it.

This woman intrigues my Soul.

I want her arms to wrap around me tightly and feel the sensation of her embrace.

Her eyes are blue, oceanic, and deep as if they have bared witness to the most challenging scenes of life and held much sorrow.

I want them to stare into my Soul and undress me from across the room.

Her hands look solid and rough as if they had worked tirelessly throughout her life.

I wanted her fingers to undress me and wrap around my hips slowly.

She holds a sense of masculine energy, but I knew there was softness under all her tough-ass persona. I wanted to touch the soft. Feel it up against me. I wanted to feel the rough too. The more I learned about her, the more I realized how we have come from completely opposite worlds in this life. Yet, she was so familiar to me. How did we know each other from before?

I wanted to know all the details of her past up to this point of meeting each other. I wanted her voice to whisper lightly and softly into my ear. This woman intrigues my Soul. She is igniting it like a hot flame. I can feel the desire start to pulse through my body.

This was the initiation to what I call, The Acceptance of Attraction. This attraction I felt in the warmth of Summer would eventually become an acceptance of my true Self in the following Season of Autumn.

FLAMES OF DESIRE

I am well into the Autumn Season. The leaves were at their peak of beauty as they would soon begin their descent onto the damp earth for a Season of rest. I was curious about the rest, too. What might that feel like for me? The air had shifted. I felt the sweet, crisp texture with each inhalation. I am managing my life to the best of my abilities: renting out three properties on Airbnb, working a full-time career, going through the Wild & Awake training program, and creating life and moments around my kids and family. All the while, I am feeling like an empty vessel.

I was gearing up for our next weekend of Wild & Awake training held on the property where I lived and managed the Airbnb rentals. This event would be called the Sacred GEO Experience and was scheduled for September 2018. The ten women would arrive during this Scorpio season, which created a flare of mystery around our gathering. This is the fourth month of training together, which has brought us into each other's worlds in an already in-depth way. We had shared so much in person through July, August, and September and through our social media group, texts, conversations, and emails. We were all excited and anticipated another great weekend of training together; however, I felt nervous about hosting this group of women at my house and property.

As I was helping set up the final details with Melissa, my friend and our group facilitator, she said to me, *"This weekend together will be intense."* I felt a giant gulp in my throat. I knew it in my bones, too. I knew that my desire had built to a level of intensity that I didn't feel I could control. I felt as if I might explode at any moment. I knew that if I didn't share the most authentic desires I was experiencing in my body and thoughts, it would eat right through my Soul. I took a deep breath and knew this was the weekend that I would speak my truth to this safe, sacred container of women.

On this Autumn morning, the temperature had dropped, the sky was grey, and a soft, gentle rain was falling. The Retrograde Ranch house on the property serves as an Airbnb rental and a yoga studio. I walked to the Ranch from my house feeling nervous and excited. All the other women seemed to be in quiet, contemplative states. As everyone created their own "nests" of yoga mats, warm and cozy blankets, journals, and hot tea, I could almost feel my heartbeat pounding out of my chest. Looking out the big windows, I let my senses immerse me in the moment: I watched the rain gently fall over the property, I felt the warmth of the candles, I inhaled the smell of the essential oils, and I listened to the sound of the calming music. I felt held and safe.

Melissa's playlist filled the room with music and emotion. We each had a large piece of paper, and there were markers and colored pencils all around us. She asked us:

"What are the DESIRES you want to bring into your life? What is your SOUL longing for in this Season of your life?"

The music, the rain, and the safety of being in a container of women who loved and supported me set the perfect stage for me to speak. Tears welled up in my eyes, and I could feel the chills up and down my spine as I feverishly wrote with my marker:

I desire to be touched and loved by a woman. I am longing for love in a new way than what I am currently receiving. I want to be filled up in a different way than what my life is holding day-to-day. I want more freedom!

The tears continued to fall on my color-filled paper, which only enlarged my desires into a more precise picture for me to see. The reality begins to sink into what I know to be true about myself. I know that I have a pattern of setting intentions that can magnificently come to fruition. So I begin asking questions: What will this mean for my future? What are these thoughts and intentions putting into action? How could my desires play out in real life – not just on paper?

In our safe space, we shared. We each took turns sharing what we were calling in. The truth was falling out of my mouth, and there was no turning back. I could not put my wishes back into my heart. I looked down at the paper. Shit. I am now witnessing my deepest desires in solid form. Have I been a fraud my whole life? How will I be able to juggle the current structure and constraints of my lifestyle with this deeper knowing that is staring back at me in my own handwriting?

Our circle concludes for the morning. We all get up to refresh our teas, take care of our needs, and pause for a break. As I moved through the space to accommodate the needs of my Sisters and myself, I was greeted in the kitchen by the one friend I was most nervous about facing. "It's going to be okay," she whispered. She leaned in to hug me, and I allowed the embrace, took a deep breath, and at this moment, I knew that she was right. I had no idea that this would become the embrace that led me to my truth of Self and the embrace that I would eventually consider *home*.

BADASS MANIFESTER

Badass Manifestor was stitched in black letters on a trucker hat that my friend Sara Beth gave me as a gift. She gave it to me at the closing ceremony of The Sacred GEO Experience. Why was this important to me?

Since my childhood, I have learned and understood the concept of manifestation as a means of spiritual practice. Whether one believes in manifestation or not, it seems to be one of the critical concepts in conscious living communities. I have read many books on manifestation and listened to many great spiritual leaders speak on the topic. One of the more significant to me was Florence Scovel Shinn, *The Game of Life and How to Play It*.

"All that we are is a result of what we have thought." ~ Buddha

I have talked with my girlfriends about being careful what you wish for and how what you set your mind to will come to fruition, so think carefully. A practice of manifestation had been well established at this time of my life, and I have been able to identify how this has played out time and time again for me in my life. If we all look back on our paths and journeys, we all should be able to see how we have created and manifested our life paths to this point. I also believe in free will. I will never agree that people generate and call tragedy, heartbreak, suffering, or trauma into their lives with their thoughts. I sit in a place of compassion and non-judgment: each person's story is valid and different. However, from my personal experience, I have found that my inner wisdom speaks to me in moments of quiet solitude. When I put my mind to something, I hear the messages of what wants to be created in my heart.

A significant example of how my life has played out in this call and response is the story of how I acquired the Retrograde Ranch house. I lived in a log cabin house, my dream home, which I built with my then-husband, next to the Retrograde Ranch. I used to run along the driveway for exercise and mainly to clear my mind and emotions. It wasn't a very long stretch of gravel road. Still, it had trees and natural foliage along the driveway. I felt very safe and secure, like I was running in a tunnel of green vegetation of Heart Chakra energy. At the end of the stretch of the driveway is a busy county road, so I would typically do a quick turn around so that I could repeat the distance a couple of times. When I would do these little turnarounds, I would always do a quick neighborly check-in on the house to the south. Knowing an elderly couple lived in this house, I was inclined to see if the house appeared okay and that nothing was alarming around it or the property.

It could have been one significant time or several, but I can recall hearing the teeny-tiny voice in my head that said, *"You will own this house one day."* And so I listened. Not knowing what the heck that meant, I brought it up to my husband on several occasions. Why in the world would we buy our neighbor's old, run-down ranch house? The idea and concept behind this made no sense to me at that moment, but I have also learned that timing is everything. I continued to honor this thought for several years as I ran every lap up and back on my driveway. My life also continued on to build a career in the family business. I became a mother, first to a baby boy and then twenty-three months later to a baby girl. I started a natural health publication in central Ohio, which I then sold to my partner a few years later. I also started the path of Spiritual/Yoga/Mindfulness retreats.

November of 2016, and several jogs up and down the driveway later, we finished cleaning up after an unbelievable feast on Thanksgiving Day with the family. With all the abundance of food, we packed up a full Thanksgiving meal and walked it down to our neighbors that lived in the Ranch house at the time. There was a new car that I had not ever seen in the driveway, which made me happy that this elderly couple had a visitor, as that was rarely the case. Their daughter answered the door and had a look of sadness and pain. I handed her the containers of food as she ungratefully shooed us away. Something wasn't right. I could tell that something terrible had happened, and my heart sunk.

The elderly woman had fallen ill and was in the hospital. That is all we could gather due to a language barrier. The family was incredibly private and was unwilling to receive any support. I was sad for her husband. He needed care, and I was not confident that he would be okay living alone. I was right.

Spring of 2017, my then-husband and I received a call from a county social worker saying he had fallen and broken his back. It was likely he was not going to survive the medical care. I continued to find ways to connect with their daughter to share my support. Although we had language as a barrier, I still cared for and looked after this elderly couple for many years while living next door to them. I felt helpless. It wasn't until the end of the Summer that we noticed movement around the house. The house looked as if it was being cleared out, and a real estate sign went into the ground. The teeny-tiny voice inside me became loud and clear, "You *must buy this house!*"

Being married to a real estate agent was a helpful factor in my story. The house was in shambles and needed a lot of work. The financials did not make any sense for us to buy it, but I was grateful that my then-husband was willing to follow my instinct on this purchase. We got a loan to buy this run-down Ranch house and some extra funds to renovate it.

The house renovation project started a new chapter in my new decade of life. At forty years old, I celebrated my birthday with family and friends in the finished garage of this house. My brother and I enjoyed all the moments before decorating and creating a charming place that I was determined would be an excellent investment for a short-term rental. Airbnb was taking off as a new and innovative platform to share and host your property, and I was excited to see where this new venture of my life was going to play out. I had no idea that the house I bought, renovated, and created for business, would eventually become my healing home, my sanctuary. This house would be the place that would hold me through the most painful seasons of my life and bring in all new moments of joy. This little house would be where I find a rebirth of who I am and how I will restart a new life for myself, my kids, and a new partner.

Oh, *this* is what it means to be a *Badass Manifester!*

Letter to the Crone, November 2020

Dearest Crone,

The weather has turned, and the chill in the air invites us to turn inward. The trees are losing their leaves and becoming barren, and the ground has hardened in preparation for the long Winter ahead. My dear Crone, may I assume you have found yourself with all the comforts to keep you cozy and warm this Season?

This is the time of year to turn inward and reflect on all we have harvested from the past Autumn Season. This Season, we honor the Spirit and archetype of the Crone. I hope this letter finds you doing well and in the space to be an open-hearted and compassionate Soul for me.

I have been evaluating my life in its entirety, taking stock of all that I have in my life, as you ask me to do each Autumn Season. I have found that I am experiencing new sensations, desires, and lust in my body that I have not ever felt before. I am awakened in the early mornings to a physical sensation that feels so intense that it causes my body to convulse with pleasure. I have read the descriptions and theories of these types of body sensations. They all lead to the concepts around the rising of Kundalini energy. These energy surges seem crazy and bizarre to me. Yet, I feel that my body has finally granted me permission to feel ecstatic pleasure in a way I have never experienced before.

I've opened up to only a few of my closest girlfriends about this happening. I also have to share that I have disclosed to the Wild & Awake training group that I genuinely desire to be touched and loved by a woman. I'm trying desperately to keep this all from my husband. I know he is curious and starting to wonder about my morning sensations. I can't tell him that I dream about women every day. I can't tell him that I have fantasized about being intimate with a woman instead of him for many years.

Oh, my dear Crone, I know you have lived through many different chapters of life and pretty much have heard it all! I hope you can hold me through this awareness and the truth that needs to come out of me. I hope you can share any wisdom about what I should do to unveil this secret I have carried with me for most of my life. I trust that your wisdom will also comfort me during this Season of my life.

Thank you, sweet Crone, for all you have given to me throughout my life and journey. I am always so grateful for your knowledge and wisdom.

Much love to you on these darkening days,

Kerry Hope

Crown Chakra: Lessons on Spiritual Connection

My Mother whispers to Me: *"Hey you. Can you just slow down for a moment so we can chat?"*

Me: (sigh) *"Yeah, what's up? I have a million things on my to-do list today, and I really don't have time to chit-chat."*

My Mother: "*I know, dear love. I know you are busting your butt right now. You are working a full-time job and side hustles, parenting two kids, doing laundry, making grocery runs, and cleaning the three short-term rentals. You are also moving your kids in and out of the house so you can Airbnb your family home... Wait... Why are you doing ALL of this again?*"

Me: "*I know, it's a lot. I'm exhausted. I am trying so hard to get ahead financially and keep up with all the demands, it is a lot, but I can do it.*"

My Mother: "*Oh honey, I know you can, but at what cost to you?*"

Me: "*I don't know. I guess I am trying to prove that I can do it all. I know I can do it all, but yeah I feel like all I am doing is constantly moving and proving.*"

My Mother: "*Okay love. Let's take a moment and pause. Can you find a moment to sit and be still? Can you find a moment to sit in the quiet with me? Come love, grab a tea, sit down in your favorite green chair and let's have a little heart to heart.*"

Me: (reluctant exhale) "*Fine, okay, tea in hand, what is that you need me to hear?*"

My Mother: "*Beautiful woman. First, thank you for taking a moment to pause and be present with me. We need to honor the time to rest. You cannot continue on this path of doing without any time to be still and quiet. Second, in these moments of stillness, quiet, and being fully present with your own thoughts, you will hear what your inner wisdom needs to share with you.*

Dear sweet Kerry Hope, you know this! You understand that the power of connection to our Divine source, our higher power of Self, is in these moments. It's okay that I have to remind you from time to time. It's okay if you neglect your spiritual practices at times because you can always come back to them. You can always find a way to pick back up where you left off in either your yoga practice, our nature walks, or in quiet reflection."

Me: "*Yes, thank you for the sweet reminders.*"

My Mother: "*As I have your attention, I need you to reflect on how you got to where you are in this life. Spend some time thinking about how you arrived here. You can do this reflection in your car while driving, or even while you are clearing a rental house, just reflect.*"

Me: "*Yeah, okay I can do that, that seems easy enough. Really, part of my spiritual practice is reflection. So I've got this, looking back on life, no problem.*"

My Mother: *"Good. Now, think back on previous times in your life when you felt the most connected to our Divine Source."*

Me: *"Oh I have always felt connected when I am surrounded by beautiful nature, either working in my recreation career or just enjoying the moments alone in nature. Yoga, of course. And mainly when I spend time thinking and reflecting, journaling and being quiet, so that my inner Self and my team of Spirit guides can cut through the noise of my ego thoughts."*

My Mother: *"That's right, love. Those are all the ways we feel into our connection to the Divine Source, which is what we believe to be our God, right? The energy you feel when you are in these moments of your life is the Crown Chakra energy that is full and connected. The energy is unblocked so that you can receive all that you need to hear, know, be reminded of, and be reassured. This is the energy you need to create for your well-being! This is how you will continue on your life path in complete alignment. You can always be connected to the universal energy of God, or as you like best to say, your Divine Source. You have shared your work through your women's circles, and the Sacred GEO Experience retreats you lead. You have taught women again and again that there is one universal energy and all creatures are connected to the same source. We are all connected.*

Please, please, don't forget how important this message is through this Season of your life. Please remember that your body is directly connected to our planet, the trees, the animals, and all the people who share this space and time with you. We are all One."

Me: *"Yes, thank you for the reminders. I do feel as if my Crown Chakra energy can get blocked, or ignored at times, especially when I am just busying myself with tasks all day."*

My Mother: *"I love you, dear sweet woman. You are doing the best that you can in this life you have created. Stay open. Stay connected to the Divine Source, and you will do just fine. You can always come back to the quiet moments, and I will be here for you. I love you."*

THE SOUL'S PATH AND FALLING IN LOVE

In my young adulthood, I fell in love with the teachings of Carolyn Myss. A great memory was listening to her speak to a large congregation of the Spiritually Unitarian Church in Naples, Florida. Carolyn Myss says her truth so frankly and assertively, and I found her intimidating at the time. However, I truly loved the teachings she shared in her books. The most poignant to me is the concept of *Sacred Contracts*. She believes that we all come into our lives with established contracts with other Souls. The theory is that we are predestined to be in a relationship with each person in our lives. All of our relationships are set up before coming into existence at birth. In essence, we sign up to learn from each of our relationships.

My mother, brother, father, cousins, aunts, uncles, grandparents, children, friends, and significant others have all been pre-established to be in each others' lives in these settings and agreed upon roles. Further, we have agreed to learn and experience lessons that our Soul has contracted to learn from each of these relationships, and each person in your life comes in for a reason. The more significant relationships and lessons come from these pertinent relationships in our daily lives: spouse, partner, mother, father, and siblings. So yes, we can choose our spouse based on human connection and attraction, but in Myss's theory, this is also a person from whom you are contracted to learn great lessons.

In addition, some of the greatest lessons I have learned were from brief interactions and relationships. Think back on all the people and interactions you have had throughout your life. Childhood friends, school teachers, dance instructors and coaches, friends from camp, co-workers, college roommates, classmates, bosses, and babysitters. Each person has provided a helpful lesson or even a significant life-changing moment.

An example of a significant sacred contract for me occurred in December of 1996. I missed my ride with friends to the Phoenix airport from Flagstaff, Arizona, where I was a student at Northern Arizona University. At the last minute, I booked a seat on a Greyhound bus arriving late that night in Phoenix, allowing me to catch my early flight the following day back to Indianapolis for Winter break. The bus came to the Oak Creek Canyon terminal, and I was eager to jump out for a quick pee and grab water. As I climbed down the bus stairs, I saw two guys off to the side smoking a cigarette. I noticed a sensation in my body as I locked eyes with one of the guys. He was taller, had broad shoulders, and was wearing glasses. His friend was sending him off on the next leg of his journey, which I remember was heading back to the East Coast.

This was when I met Israel, an incredibly handsome traveling vagabond who intentionally chose the open seat next to me. Serendipitously meeting each other on this bus ride leads to an all-night dinner at a hotel near the airport. We sat outside by the hotel pool, ate grilled cheese, and drank mug after mug of tea, keeping us caffeinated into the wee hours of the morning. We learned about each other's past nineteen and twenty years of life and held so much interest and respect, which continued into a sweet, romantic love. He and I exchanged handwritten letters and occasional phone calls for months. I even took a road trip out to North Carolina from Indiana to see him while he was on break from basic training at Camp LaJune in the fall of 1997. Our interactions together during this chapter of my life were nothing but sweet, romantic affection. It felt like something you would have watched unfold in a movie.

Then one day, the relationship just stopped. We realized that our sacred contract with each other was complete. There were no hard feelings or deep sadness, and there wasn't a sense of relief. It was just time to move in new directions. I love all the moments I shared with Israel, and I hold all the memories of our time together as sacred. But, mainly, I love that meeting Israel is a perfect example of how people come into your life, even if for a brief time. Being consciously aware of all the people in your life can open up more awareness to how all of your relationships are truly sacred contracts. All these short-lived experiences with these different people are predestined and purposeful for me in this life. All the connections were significant, needed, and necessary in allowing me to end up here, where I am today.

Looking back now, I see how much I have learned from each significant player in my life. A beautiful way to honor this for yourself is to open your journal and write out each family and closest friend's name in a list, leaving space. Then in sweet contemplation, go through and write next to each person what they have taught you. What influence have they made on your personal development? What lessons have you learned from each person? (Hint, hint: They will likely not even know what all they have provided to you and for you.) This exercise is a powerful process, and it often takes time to feel into all the lessons. Some of this can bring up some painful memories. As we may all know, love can be painful too. I contribute my spiritual path and awareness to a conscious, open heart through many challenging conversations and moments with my family and friends. In these conversations, we are "doing the work."

When I see how the major players in my life have provided me with love and lessons, I sit in a place of gratitude for each person.

Thank you.

Thank you to my family, closest friends over the years, and my once-husband. He and I shared one of the most significant relationships of laughter and joy I have ever experienced. In our time, we created a life of adventure, and many celebratory moments, bringing two baby humans into the world together. I will forever honor all the beautiful good moments we shared. I will also forever keep sacred all that I have learned from him and all that I was able to learn about myself. I will celebrate falling in love and honor falling out of love. We were destined to be in each other's lives for two decades as a married couple, mother and father to our children, and best friends to each other. As we have moved out of the role as husband and wife, I will always honor our relationship. We continue to find more lessons even as we navigate as co-parents to our children. I guess you can say the learning doesn't stop even after a change in the relationship.

I have always loved the photos in the newspapers announcing an elder couple celebrating their sixty-seventh wedding anniversary together. The look on their faces, worn out and tired on the outside, yet this feeling of accomplishment in their eyes that only Olan Mills photography can capture. Being in love and dedicated to another person, the amount of love, laughter, heartbreak, and tears that these two beings have endured over a lifetime is truly a remarkable feat.

How did these two people meet? What is their story of falling in love together? And how did that love remain so vital for all these years? How much did they learn from each other?

I have a hard time believing that we have one Soul Mate in each lifetime. However, I respect the people who fall in love with one person and commit each day and night for their lifetimes. I think it's magical. These couples have contracted to be in each other's lives for such a magnificent amount of time together.

I believe that my Soul has fallen in and out of love with many different people. I have fallen in love with several other women at different points in my life who then became my closest friend, sister, and best friend. The mere act of falling in love over and over should be our most significant accomplishment as humans. We have the exceptional capability of falling in love with multiple people and throughout our lives with many different people. However, there is conditioning placed on us that we are only allowed to have one person to love forever and ever. Geesh. Think about all the love you could miss out on if you only choose one person.

If we were to look at our ability to love with open hearts, perhaps it could shift how we view so many relationships in our lives. There are male friends that I have had throughout the years too. Guys who are so funny and would bring me laughter until I peed my pants. Guys with whom I shared moments of adventure and care-taking young campers as we trekked through the wilderness as co-leaders and guides. Guys who I share love and admiration with for my best friends as they engage in marriage or partnership. I never engaged in nor felt any sexual chemistry with these men. I just genuinely fell in love with them as a people. My Soul LOVES to fall in love!

I look at the theories of Carolyn Myss with the understanding that we are contracted to love certain people. These Souls are to come into our lives to teach us what our lessons are in each lifetime. When I look at these theories in this way, having multiple Soul Mates feels right for me.

I have gained all that I could from my relationship and marriage to my once husband. When I found myself falling in love with another Soul, an additional Soul Mate that was a different gender this time, I couldn't help but reflect on my earlier learning of our Sacred Contracts. So what is this new chapter, Season, relationship, and the person going to teach me? How can I contemplate the devastation of a marriage ending and see it as beautiful at the same time? How can I hold gratitude in my heart for all the memories? How can I honor all the lessons I learned from my marriage?

THE TRAIL OF INTUITIVE CRUMBS

As a person who chooses to live a spiritually alive life path, I have never doubted any synchronicities in my life. I have retraced the bread crumbs on my life journey over and over again. I am often recapping the trail of my life to revisit how far I have traversed.

One example of this type of life path recapping can sound like this:

"Well, if I didn't end up going out west to college, I would have never met my friend Roxanne. She invited me to work the Summer camp job in Pebble Beach, California, with her family. I experienced so many incredible outdoor adventures and beauty in the Big Sur region and met Adena. Adena then ended up taking me to Stanford University so I could work another camp gig to finish out my Summer. That is where I met Nickie, who is still one of my best friends twenty-five years later. If I didn't experience that week at Stanford, I wouldn't have grown to love all the aspects of recreation and camp management and changed my area of study at Indiana University. I finished off my education in Indiana and raced back to California to do my internship again at the same camp program at Stanford, which is where I met my future husband."

As I rewind my mind to see how I followed the breadcrumbs throughout my life, I am reassured that the trail always seems to serve me in some capacity. I don't know if it is merely confirmation that I was on the "Right Path" in life, but what if we all took more time to notice how one decision leads to the next? Acknowledging the unfolding of our lives could bring more awareness of how one decision leads to the next. I find the synchronicities along the way to be poignant in my life regardless. And many would agree that not all of my life has been forged by significantly great decisions.

If you take the time to reflect on your past, it can bring more awareness to where you are now. What were the factors that led you to your decisions? Were you guided by knowledgeable parents, or did you follow your siblings' steps? If we live more consciously, we often are guided by our inner knowledge. Our intuition allows us to traverse from chapter to chapter and Season to Season in our lives. When we look back on our journeys in life and then choose to live a more aware, open-hearted, conscious life, it is imperative to find quiet solitude to listen to our hearts.

The decisions I have made and the times of saying *yes* were a matter of following my intuition. Listening and feeling into my gut always leads me to the next crumb to follow. For instance, my inner wisdom knew that I wanted to submerge myself into a more profound training long before I decided to enroll in the Wild & Awake program. This yearning was waiting in my heart in the cold months of Winter. On a snowy morning in January 2019, I spoke about this desire to my close friends, Erica and Melissa. We sat together curled under blankets, sipping hot coffee in our cabin overlooking the land and waters in Michigan. I couldn't decide if I was meant to go through a YTT (Yoga Teacher Training) or if I would find a Guru in the hills of the Himalayan mountains. Still, I knew that I wanted to ask deeper questions of myself and find other answers about how I could live a more conscious and purpose-filled life.

I brought this up as a way of me merely laying down a bread crumb. A few weeks later, Melissa and Erica created what was conceptualized as Wild & Awake Goddess Circle Training. Women empower themselves and each other through yoga, meditation, and learning about life around the Wheel of the Year. This was just the beginning of the synchronicities that would forever change me and the beautiful unfolding of my life path. I was meant to live in sync with the Seasons of the year and allow my transition to this new way of life.

I continue to find and follow the intuitive bread crumbs that I drop for myself or the ones that the great Universe lays out before me. But, living in truth, living awake and conscious, allows the synchronicities to flourish and grow. So for me, being open and curious about what lies ahead on my journey and finding the balance to stay present in my current moments is how I find my way. This is the dance I choose to create and participate in every day.

My center point of Self always comes back to my gratitude practice. Are you taking time to reflect on all that has served you in your life thus far? Are you thankful for all the people you have encountered along the way? How are you meandering down the path of life: are you picking up bread crumbs along the way, or are you dropping them so others could find you?

The Trail of Intuition and being connected to your higher source, whatever that may be for you, is a beautiful gift you can offer yourself.

MY THANKSGIVING PRAYER

Full of beautiful gifts waiting to be shared, my abundant heart expands beyond any realm I've encountered. I am finding corners of depth in each chamber that have yet to be discovered. I allow the expression of love in the new ways that my Soul desires.

My abundant heart, so sweet and fragile, is willing to take the risks of being shattered to have just one more moment in time with you. I am exposing my Soul – naked, raw – to have one more moment of giving my love to you.

I am awake in my wildness, clear and free, and know that challenging the cosmos and destiny is a battle not for the weak.

I am reminded with great frequency of what I love the most. These sensations of love. The feelings of desire and longing, lust, and euphoria. My Soul is reminded of the possibilities. My body is reminded of the aches. My heart is reminded of the limitless terrain. What I love the most is loving you.

Thank you, body.

Thank you, Soul.

Thank you.

This is my Thanksgiving Prayer to you.

CONNECTING TO YOUR OWN MOTHER AND CRONE WISDOM: VISUALIZATION

Before you read this next section, please find yourself in a place of peace and solitude. Have a journal and pen nearby (or use this book to jot down any notes) so that you may capture any wisdom you gain as you connect to your inner knowing from your Mother and Crone archetypes.

Pause now to close your eyes, and take three slow, deep, long, rich breaths in and out.

As you settle into yourself, begin by noticing all your sensations around your body. What does your clothing feel like on your skin? Are you warm, or is there a chill in the air? What smells do you notice around you? How does this book feel in your hands or on your lap? Step yourself through all five senses of your Being.

How, at this moment, are you caring for your personal needs? Adjust yourself accordingly, and provide any additional comforts for yourself. Are your toes covered with cozy socks or a blanket? Do your shoulders feel wrapped up and secure? Or do you need a gentle breeze of a fan to keep you cool?

You are the most faithful, most magnificent Mother to yourself. You are able to provide the same sense of warmth as one might feel from a grandmother's embrace and a small kiss on the head. Our own tenderness can be felt in how we pay attention to all that we do for ourselves. Your Mother is within you now. Your Grandmother is within you now.

At this moment, you are able to feel the love surrounding your Being, and you notice a sound of cackling laughter off in the distance. This strikes your curiosity, and so you follow the sound. You continue to hear the laughter get louder, and you begin to head out toward the back of your space. You open the door to the outside and are greeted with a crisp gentle breeze in the air. This creates a little zip of energy in your body, as both the cool air and louder sounds of laughter startle you.

You continue to venture out into the open space, and now you smell the smoke of a fire mixed in with the aroma of pine and damp earth. You follow the sounds of two women's voices and the fantastic smell of firewood burning in the Autumn air. As you eagerly start to pick up your pace, you turn the corner around a bushel of dried, pale yellow grasses and find two beautiful women sitting in large, brown Adirondack chairs. One has mid-length hair, brushing down over her shoulders and covered with a red scarf around her neck. The other woman is slightly older, with silver streaks of greyish-white hair draped down over her black, wool-woven cloak wrapped tightly around her body.

They turn their heads to greet you. *"Hello, darling. Glad you decided to join us,"* Says the Mother. *"We have been enjoying our moments catching up on all the greatness we have witnessed in your life."* The Crone speaks in a soft voice. *"Please come sit and join us by this warm fire."*

As you move toward the bonfire, you notice the three chairs form a crescent moon, and there is an empty space in the middle waiting for you. On this chair sits a beautiful woven blanket with red, black, and white markings making a beautiful pattern. As you sit, you notice the intricacies of these patterns and graciously wrap this blanket around your lap. You feel an overwhelming sense of love and protection surrounding you now as you stare into the flames of the fire.

Mother speaks: *"You sit in a beautiful space in your life right now my dear. Even if you feel overwhelmed, even if you feel anxious at times, or unsure about certain aspects of your daily life, you are doing exceptionally well just being you."*

These words settle into your heart, and you feel your eyes start to swell slightly with tears. You had been craving a little love and validation for your Soul. These words mean everything to you at this moment.

The Crone woman reaches her hand over to your leg, gently placing it on your covered knee.

"You, my dear, have so much love and wisdom in your heart. Please do not let the darkness of doubt ever take away what you already know to be true. You are doing a beautiful job navigating some really hard things in this life, and please know that your Mother and I are here through this Season of Life with you every step of the way."

Mother and Crown, together: *"In this season, we want you to remember . . ."*

What do they say to you now?

Listen.

A slight smile appears across your face. You look at your Mother and your Crone with appreciative eyes, sharing all the gratitude for their time and wisdom. You reach over to grab the soft, wrinkly hands of the older woman, holding them gently within your hands. What do you want to say to her now?

Then, you stand up and lean in to hug her as she remains comfy in her chair. You turn to the other woman, your Mother. She sprouts right up out of her chair to embrace you. She tilts her head and smiles with so much love for you. As you embrace, what is it that comes from your heart to share with her now?

You gently place your beautiful blanket down on the chair and head back toward the path that brought you to the bonfire. As you are walking back to your space, you wrap your arms around yourself to keep the warmth of the fire and the love you received tightly around your chest.

What are you feeling at this moment?

Do you hear any words or phrases that stand out to you from either your Mother or your Crone?

What does your inner Mother want you to know? Is she proud of you? Does she have suggestions on how you can better take care of or nurture yourself? Is there anything you felt you needed to say back to her?

How was it to hear your wise words from your own inner Crone? Was she able to offer support and guidance to you for where you are currently at on your life path? Did you find yourself saying anything in response to your Crone's wisdom or advice?

When you return to your place of comfort, grab your journal and write down all the messages, wisdom, insights, stories, and memories that you received in this time of reflection. You can repeat this visualization as many times as you like allowing your inner Mother and inner Crone to speak to you. Anytime throughout your day, you can simply take some deep breaths, close your eyes and ask, "Mother, I could use your support at this time." And then simply pose your question. The answers always lie within.

II

THE SEASON OF WINTER

HONORING YOUR DIVINE CONNECTION

In Winter, we feel a sense of completion to all we have created. Our smiles soften, our feet and hands slow down, and we begin to tuck our bodies into softness and warmth.

We use our shortened days to maximize our steadiness.

We use our longer nights to deepen rest in our bodies.

Winter brings the calm our Souls long for throughout the year. Winter gives us all the permission to feel into our comforts. What are your non-negotiable comforts in this Season? What elements of your environment bring your body, mind, and Soul the peace you desire?

Finding comfort for yourself in the Winter Season is a form of beautiful creative expression that soothes and honors your need for rest. This expression of yourself allows you to create softness for your Being in your own home and allows your body to feel safe, secure, held, and loved.

In our modern culture, we are taught to believe that rest is a pleasure and must be earned. Rest is something you should only do once you are no longer living. So for many of us, the very act of rest and restoring ourselves can lead to thoughts and unconscious emotions of not being worthy of this human need. When we can honor the rest in this Season, we are forgiving ourselves for all that we are not doing—forgiving ourselves for all that we are not achieving and releasing the guilt around the need not to strive. Thank yourself for all that you have accomplished up to this point.

When we slow down and focus on a single moment, we notice what our heart asks for in this quiet Season. Listen softly to hear the tiny "yes, thank you" as you put on your favorite wool socks or knit sweater. Notice your smile as you tuck your legs and arms into your beloved sofa blanket —the scent of your Winter potpourri, candle, and brewed tea. Soften, dear one. Allow the exhale to lengthen and feel the softness of your Soul.

These are the moments when the Divine sits with you in the silence of the snowfall. These are the moments when you can commune with your Divine Spirit through walks in the Winter parks or woodlands as you listen to the sound of your feet moving on your daily walk with your pup. Allowing this connection will bring you the peace we all strive to find. Find your peace.

Hush your mind. Thank yourself for all the work you've done. Rest, dear one. Rest.

Crown Chakra: Lessons on the Journey

My Crone whispers to Me: *"Well, you are up early this morning, my dear. Trouble sleeping?*

Me: *"Oh, yeah, sorry if I woke you too. I was just going to sit in my favorite green chair and read, think, or something. But, yeah, it's been hard for me to sleep lately. So I am finding the quiet moments to soothe my heart."*

My Crone: *"Do you mind if I join you on this chilly morning. I love to enjoy every moment of these colder months. This time of year is my favorite to wake early and snuggle with a warm tea."*

Me: *"Sure! I would love your company. But, hey, remember the last conversation we held right here in the kitchen about finding more time and devotion to connecting with my Divine source?"*

My Crone: *"Well, yes, of course, dear, I remember all of our conversations, and yes, I have been witnessing you making a great effort, such as using this time in the early morning to be present with yourself. Do you feel you are opening up the Crown energy and connection?"*

Me: (Sigh) *"I don't know, I guess I am. I'm struggling with all that is going on in my life right now. I am incredibly overwhelmed and riddled from head to toe with anxiety. My heart feels like it is cracking open or apart. I don't know which. I am trying to stay grounded in all the ways, and I even borrowed a grounding mat from a friend and have been sitting on it to help regulate my energetic fields. I am trying everything I can, but I am struggling. I am not clear if I am hearing my inner wisdom speaking or if my connection to my higher source is working. I'm desperately trying to find a resolution to this situation I am in."*

My Crone: *"Yes, dear one, I can see that you are sitting on volatile ground right now. I can sense how much anxiety this has caused. I see your body is rebelling too, and your physical body even broke out in shingles—poor dear. But, I can also see that you are doing your best to get through this period of your life that you are calling the In-Between."*

Me: *"Yes, that's the only way I can describe this chapter of my life."*

My Crone: *"I see. Yes, that seems to suit well for a description. However, I also see what you may not; your Divine guides or Spirit guides are helping you in every moment of every day. Keeping your heart open to hearing or seeing the signs they are showing, you will get you through this In-Between."*

Me: *"I know, I know, but I feel like I am missing their guidance or I am looking too hard for clues. I just need to know what I should do next."*

My Crone: *"Oh, my dear sweetheart, I can feel your panic. I know you are stressed. Take a deep breath, take heart. You are doing the very best you can do right now. Finding time to sit in peace, writing out your feelings in your journal, including all you are afraid of losing, continue to take one more step each day. Your guides will bring you the best possible timing so that you can continue to take the next best step for you, your kids, and your family.*

Keep trusting, love. Keep trusting."

FAITH AND TRUST IN THE DIVINE: THE ANCIENT RUINS

The Season was Winter, but we were in the heat of the sun. The heat of the Mexican mountain terrain. The ghosts of the Mesoamerican ancestors stood as witnesses on our family vacation. The first day of the 2020 decade. The day of wrecking a marriage that was almost at the nineteenth year mark.

The moment of truth.

The moment of truth.

The moment.

The words came out of my mouth without rehearsal. The needs and desires that were longing inside. The explanation of why I haven't been acting myself lately. I found all the ways around the actual fact of what was happening—finding the courage. "Keep going," I heard a little voice.

The tower crumbled.

The tower crumbled.

The tower.

The color of his face turned pale. *"Is there someone else?"* I heard the words, and my brain couldn't find a way to work around the question. "Yes."

Praying for Forgiveness.

Praying for Forgiveness.

Praying.

Based on all the emotions felt, we shared the palpable pain. I knew that the only way to get to the other sides of this was to walk right through. I knew that owning my truth was going to be painful. I knew that my choices were going to have repercussions. I knew that I had to bury myself in the only thing I had left inside: my faith.

Trust the Divine.

Trust the Divine.

Trust.

THE IN-BETWEEN

There I sat, in the snuggly sweetness of Sisterhood and the saltiness of tears and truth on a dark, rainy Winter day of Wild & Awake Training. I leaned in to hear, feel, and be present to each of my Wild Sister's stories and my own in the Storytelling portion of our training. I told a story of my life as a woman married to a man for nearly nineteen years – the story that I thought would be my happily ever after. I knew, though – even as the words spilled out of my mouth – that this would be the last time I would speak this version of my story. This story, this version, this understanding of how I perceive my life's path and journey as I have known it for almost forty-three years is changing into something different.

In-Between.

The phase of the *In-Between* for me started around the middle of December 2019, and the concept became very clear to me. I was holding two different stories, realities, lives, and loves. I witnessed myself move from one cocoon to building and weaving another. Living in duality and the *In-Between*. The duality of ALL knowing and all that I knew. The duality of the unknown and certainty. The duality of truth and lies. The *In-Between* contained moments of complete euphoria, light, love, and connection beyond and beyond. Feeling strength in all-knowing of Self while at the same time completely second-guessing everything I ever knew.

I knew in my bones there was no turning back to the story I had been telling. No turning back to what existed before the *In-Between*.

I have everything I need: the tools, the devotion, the strength. I have the most incredible woman by my side. I have passion, beauty, love, and power holding my hand as I walk through this uncertainty.

I thought I had the most incredible man by my side. Steady, compassionate, loving, devoted.

I am walking through the fire. Knowing the fire is what will get me through this *In-Between*.

So, I take my first step.

I disclose to my husband of almost twenty years that I feel, sit, and embrace my sexuality in a new, more vital way. I feel my desires evolving. I know with everything in me that I now need a woman sexually, emotionally, and spiritually. I say nothing to the fact that I have already found Her.

But then, the conversation moves to the truth.

She already exists. I have feelings for this woman that are beyond words. I have not yet found how to say the words I am feeling. I am madly in love. I am so madly in love with this woman that I'm willing to sit in this pain, mine and his, to find a way to unravel our 18 years of marriage. I feel so strongly about this connection that I will sit in this pain of existence to witness the hurt in his eyes, watch the tears fall down his face, and feel the magnitude of the look of terror staring me down.

I hold his hand, and we continue to take little, tiny baby steps. We looked back at moments of our time together, and we reminisced on how we fell in love and how far it got us. We cried together, yelled, and clenched our jaws. Jackal voices came out in late-night whispers. We hugged. We stared at each other in the eyes, hoping an answer or resolution would come. We talked. We talked. We walked.

The process fatigue began to set into our bones. I had to physically chop carrots while seeing the man I have loved for two decades find the strength to mend back his broken heart. Piece by piece. He began working with a spiritual counselor. She coached him along the way. How to deal with his anxiety and PTSD (Post Traumatic Stress Disorder). The pain, the anger, the fear, the loneliness, the heartache, and how to survive in this *In-between*.

He began a meditation practice, a little asana in the mornings. He cleaned up his diet and started losing excessive weight. He bought a journal to write down all his emotions day-to-day, which was a safe place to process his thoughts. He began to ask more questions about my spiritual practices and the Wild & Awake training. He worked to try and catch up on a path I have been on for many years. He wants to catch up, desperately. He is opening his heart and his mind so much. He has realized that he has been going through his life in a way he thought would never change. And now, here he is standing in rubble, trying to figure out how he can plant new seeds in the stone-filled dirt.

I prayed and prayed, and I continue to pray for him.

As I sit in this *In-Between*, I continue to hold space, conversations, and visions around what could be. I envision all the delicate hearts surrounding me, and I walk carefully around each one, making sure I make no drastic movements. Making sure I choose my words with honesty and integrity. I'm living moment to moment and day to day. Time is an illusion to me now. The minutes seem like an eternity. The waiting for the healing process to move to fruition and the longing to be in Her arms again. All of this, and yet here we sit in only the fourth week of this massive life transition. So much has happened. So much has been said, and so many tears have fallen.

I ride through the peaks and valleys of emotions, thoughts, and processes. One moment, I am in relief that this is all going to work out, that I can spend my moments living in both the greatness of my mundane life and the euphoria of feeling love and lust. Then, the next day, there is an ask to eliminate this Soul connection to Her. It was causing my heart to shatter, crumbling to the floor in panic and tears. However, I am honoring the relationship I have been devoted to while also honoring myself, desires, and truth. All the while knowing that the very heart attached to my Soul mate is also hurting, broken, confused—knowing that I can't be there to embrace and support Her in her pain. This pattern continues.

So where from here? I know this. I am using the inspiration from the Aquarius season to pull back the lens to see the whole, big, beautifully messy picture. I am grounding my energy like a pro: cleaning and clearing from alcohol, increasing sleep and restoration, moving my body in more yoga, meditation to feel into my chakras, writing, eating grounding foods, and giving myself as much space as possible. I am connecting with my kids, walking the property, and tackling a "to do" list that has built up over the past three months.

The only solution to this midlife awakening is time. So I am honoring the time it will take to rebuild a solid foundation with my husband. It will take time to sit with a therapist to walk me through my next steps. Time to continue to feel, embrace and harness the Kundalini rising. As I sit in this glitter globe, I welcome the spectrum of sensations. I carefully watch each piece of glitter as it drifts down to the Earth. I honor the Divine for shaking up my globe, my world, and my knowing. I am honored to feel the truth of who I am and what my Soul calls. And once all this glitter has settled, I see myself standing there in my power. Strong, beautiful, sexy, confident in who I am. I see myself as a leader to many others who need support and guidance through their Awakenings, too.

This year is the year, now is the time. We are all called to stand in our truths. To create new stories and establish our new existence. I see myself standing openly in love, next to the most beautiful woman, hand in hand, and sharing our story. Our experience of walking the path with the Divine shows the world the greatness that we have together as a couple.

My heart is wide open with hope-filled possibilities, and my heart is open to receiving and giving so much love. The flow of love moves in and out. There is no room for fear in this flow.

I am Kerry Hope, and I am Wild & Awake, and I am here.

LOWEST POINT OF THE JOURNEY: MOTHER GUILT AND SHAME

My husband and I sat down with my mother to share our news regarding the devastating state of our marriage. We shared how things were quickly falling apart and how we were seeking her wisdom as our family's wise Crone and matriarchy.

I was lost.

My Soul was searching and needed all love and assurance that things would be okay, especially from the one person who was my best friend and provided years of counsel for me as a Mother. The news of this was shocking, of course. To say we caught her off guard would be a tad understated. She quickly responded with her sentiments of sadness and, of course, words of encouragement for us to find a way to work it out. Divorce was not an option.

In my mind, I initiated this messy situation; however, my Soul had known otherwise. I knew a profound truth was on the verge of surfacing. My truest inner knowing allowed me to feel his pain so that I was prepared for the amount of pain and heartache I was about to endure on my own.

The loss of love can be the most painful experience the human heart can feel. I have felt this only a few times in my life. The pain I was feeling and the sadness of betraying my husband was raw and real. However, when I reviewed the levels of pain and sorrow, the lowest point of this journey happened when I sat at the hotel lobby restaurant in the freezing rain of March to meet my mother and brother about my failed marriage situation. There were big objects on the walls staring at me as I sat across the table from my family on this cold, dark Winter night.

The server came and went.

Food was delivered.

My table mates ate.

I only was able to witness my tears fall into a plate of noodles, and vegetables, maybe.

The words were spoken.

The disbelief shocked me awake like a cold glass of water.

Threats were made. Altercations were placed on and around me.

My truth was non-existent and invalidated.

Shame laid on me like a cold, wet blanket.

I remember hearing words spoken as I sat in a chair, trying to keep myself from detaching my body. The words cut into my Soul, and I was dizzy. I was frozen but ready to fight or run if I needed to. I was in a state of survival in one of the most challenging conversations I have felt with the people I loved most.

"You are not gay. Lesbians love to try and steal away married women from their husbands. This is just a game."

"If you don't stay in your marriage, then there will be consequences and restructuring of the family business."

"You have fallen into the mindset of a Cult in your training program."

"It doesn't matter that you are not sexually attracted to your husband. People stay in marriages for the kids. That's the right thing to do."

I sat there with my eyes gazing down on the untouched noodles. I couldn't even form words in response. So instead, I ate the opinions, beliefs, and disapproval that I was served. I let this hurtful nourishment soak through my skin and down to the bone marrow. The people I counted on to be supportive, helpful, loving, and kind have betrayed me. Is this my karmic debt for my affair? Did I deserve this pain? Am I not worthy of being truthful and feeling my emotions?

I was numb. That night, the car ride was silent except for the cold, freezing rain pelting the windshield. Finally making it home, I paid the babysitter, changed my clothes, crawled into my daughter's bed with her to watch a movie, and fell asleep.

THE COURAGE OF THE WINTER SEED

The next day, I lay on the cold, damp earth near my home. My entire body felt shattered, disembodied, numb. I could hear the sounds of nature, birds chirping in trees that surrounded me, the scent of composted leaves that had laid in their fallen spaces through cold days and freezing nights for several months. My eyes were so swollen from tears and crusted with salt that squinting was the only option. I felt utterly broken. I laid on the ground and prayed my body would just sink into the earth's core, never having to get up ever again. Moments went by. Then I heard the voice I had known as my husband for almost two decades of my life call out to the back property on which I laid. Lunch. Food. Children. Family. The existence in my day-to-day life still beckons me. Not sure how I was going to continue, I sat up.

What I knew to be true regarding safety, security, and unconditional love was completely stripped away from my existence. Throughout my life, love surrounded me even in my darkest of times: losing my father at the age of fifty-eight to cancer when I was five weeks postpartum, the loss of grandparents, pets, lovers, and friends throughout my life. Yet, I could still manage through acceptance and healing until this particular night.

The sensation struck my lungs like jumping into a pool of icy water. I felt the pains of trauma in my heart. The pains of trauma I have worked tirelessly to heal and forgive. These pains of disapproval, rejection, shame, guilt, and invalidation will be carried along for the next few seasons of my life. I learned how to find space for their existence in my skin. The scars will shimmer when the light strikes them just right, only as a testament to myself that I will never invalidate my children's feelings and experiences with such hateful words and emotions, regardless of whether or not I agree with their choices.

This pain was as heavy as a pile of dark, dense composted soil waiting to nourish the earth. The Winter Season brings a daily reminder to me that certain processes cannot happen in the Winter. The ground cannot absorb the fresh pile of compost these days. Certain processes can only occur over time.

In the darkness of Winter, we have to also hold steady and reserve our strength. At the right moment, we can slowly stretch out our arms and legs, like coming out of Savasana at the end of a warm, yummy, yin yoga class. Winter is the time for long, deep breaths and slow, nurturing movements. Take your sweet time. Spend a little extra time doing your day-to-day routine and slowly adding new events into your schedule.

My favorite comparison is looking at the growth and resilience of a plant seed. All Winter long, the seeds lay dormant and resting. All the while, they grow their strength and build up vitality.

Then, the little seed starts to sprout an itty-bitty tiny shoot at the perfect timing. Ever so sweetly, the seed holds a gentle pace. The seed doesn't expect to become a tree overnight. And then, when the seed feels ready, and the timing is right, the momentum of our planet's energy will find the courage, passion, and drive to shoot! The growth of this seed pushes through the final layer of soil to be exposed for the world to see! This tiny seed may have driven through hard frozen ground, rocky terrain, or even through the most microscopic crack of a concrete slab. Regardless of the resistance these little seeds experience, they persevere.

I knew I was underground energetically, emotionally buried. Like a seed, I could feel the weight of the heavy frozen soil laying on top of me. I knew I had created a mess of my life and existence, but I knew I had the courage to sprout from this point. I knew I dared to persevere. So until I was ready to shoot out of the earth, I laid there dormant. I used all the energy from Mother Earth to soak into my Soul, heart, and mind. I turned the grounding energy into the vitality and courage I knew I would need to sprout.

Letter to the Crone, March 2020

Dearest Crone,

May this note of gratitude be a warm welcome into your heart on this cold, frozen Winter day. As I sit down to write the words I want to say to you, I find it hard to express how incredibly grateful I am for your love and support.

Thank you for showing up for me on the day I believed I could not make it any further in the journey of transition. The pain was unbearable for me to manage. I can only imagine how difficult it must have been for you to witness me shattered in pieces on the ground that Winter day. Yet, I know the gift we inherit as Mothers and Crones is to feel into all the joys and pains of our children. I know this to be true with my two beautiful children daily.

That day of reckoning, the day of immense pain, will be one I will never forget. The betrayal of love, the shaming, and the invalidation from my mother were more painful than I have ever endured. And, as I wept out all the pain of grief and shame, you walked down the sunlit path and found me lying on the cold ground, a complete wreck. You still showed up for me. Your words of encouragement meant everything. I will forever hear your voice and wisdom in my head and heart that day.

"Don't give up Kerry Hope. Take as long as you need to get up off the ground. Soak the earth with your tears and sorrows, these are the waters that nourish the ground, and Mother Earth can compost your sadness to create beautiful, new energy for the birds and the trees. Your own Crone Self & Mother Earth are holding you in this very moment, sweet one. The pain in your heart shall not be a waste. Do not brush it off so quickly. Feel your pain in your heart and your body, for this too will be composted into beautiful, new energy for the birds and the trees. These pains are the wisdom only your Soul can handle at this point in your life. Take your time. Breathe in the cold, damp earth and the smell of composted leaves, and when you are ready, you will rise again."

In my mind, I heard the sound of your walking stick shuffling around and your feet slowly moving back down the path where you found me—lying in the woods, body weak, eyelids crusted. I followed your advice. My body was still numb and empty. I knew that my desire to be loved and accepted by all the people in my life was not going to be easy. At that moment, I realized that if my mother could turn her back on me as I reclaimed a new love in my life, then the climb ahead would be treacherous and painful.

Then you showed up for me as a Wise Crone, and you continued to do so every day. So I knew that the wisdom we carry, the years of life experiences, and the lifetime of lessons, would enable me to get through this significant life transformation. I knew that I had all the wisdom, love, and acceptance for Myself, the love of my Maiden Self, my Mother Self, and of you, the Wise Crone. I knew that if I didn't

show up for myself, and if we didn't show up for each
other, then there was no one else that would ever be
able to love me in the future. And so I got up off
the ground and found the path back to my home.

Thank you from the bottom of my heart and Soul. I am
forever grateful for your wisdom.

Kerry Hope

Root Chakra: Lessons on the Journey

My Mother whispered to Me: *"Kerry Hope? (pause) Kerry Hope?"*

Me: *"Yeaah?"*

My Mother: *"I see you are laying on the ground again. Can I help pick you up?"*

Me: *"I'm not really in the mood for a pep talk right now, lady. My whole world is crumbling around me, and I can't move. I can't think, I can't do anything except just lay here."*

My Mother: *"Then I will lay here, right next to you. I will meet you in your space of discomfort and pain. That's what 'Mothers' do, right?"*

Me: *"I don't know anymore. I am so lost, broken, depressed, riddled with shame and guilt. My body just can't move."*

My Mother: *"So then we will work on doing whatever it takes to help you get back up when you are ready. Sound good?"*

Me: *"I don't know. I mean I am such a horrible person, I don't think I am even deserving of getting up off the floor."*

My Mother: *"Okay, lady, now come on. What is all this victim talk about? You know that you are going through an incredibly challenging time in your life. You are making the decision to find a different and perhaps a better way of life for yourself, so stop playing the 'poor me victim card'. What was Glennon Doyle's main message from her book UNTAMED?"*

Me: (sigh) *"We can do hard things."*

My Mother: *"I know that book stirred up a lot of emotions and feelings for you, listening to other women speak their truths and follow their paths can be incredibly triggering to your emotions, but I keep repeating this phrase over and over so that you can be reminded of this exact message. YOU can do hard things, Kerry Hope."*

Me: (grumbling) *"Ugh, I know this. I just don't know which hard thing I should choose? Leave a marriage or leave the love I have always wanted in my life."*

My Mother: *"Well, as you are already aware, you are going to have to follow your inner knowing, your heart, and trust your Divine Source has a plan already laid out for you. I know you have been working with your Crone archetype on your upper chakra energies: Third Eye and Crown, now you need to drop down into your Root Chakra and get to work. This is the blocked energy you are feeling at the base of your spine. So come on now, I need you to sit up. Sit on your butt, and let's focus on the base of your entire chakra energetic structure."*

Me: (more grumbling) *"Okay, fine. Are you happy? I'm sitting up."*

My Mother: *"Now take a deep breath and let's do a visualization to help open up your Root Chakra energy, lady. You will need this open energy to get through this 'hard thing.'"*

DUALITY OF LOSS: LOSING THE LIFE I BUILT AND BUILDING THE LIFE I WANTED

I had to end the relationship. My husband and family demanded that I end my love affair; it sounded like the right thing to do. And yet, there I sat, paralyzed in fear and confusion. All the years of conditioning, believing that I had to commit to only one person for my entire life. Why, then, did I stand witness to our culture and society where 59% of marriages end with a divorce.

The request to end this relationship was heart-wrenching. I had fallen in love with a woman that brought me a euphoric sense of connection, passion, and purpose. A woman who lit my Soul and Self, and who listened to me with full attentiveness and allowed me to feel my worthiness and the permission to be my powerful and healthy Self. On the other hand, there is a man, two beautiful kids, a house, a family, years of history, laughter, and plans of a shared life together, security—all that we had created in our home, our careers, our savings, our investments. So there I sat in a duality of loss. Lose my lover and the truest knowing of myself I have ever felt, or lose my life as I had known it for twenty years - my kids, my family, my income, my home, and what seemed like everything else.

All I felt was fear. Paralyzing daily fear. I learned that fear could show up in all kinds of body sensations. I had learned to adapt. The sensations of fear would cycle through my body from my womb, up to my belly, then up to my chest and heart, and then strangle my throat. Fear was really good at skipping around my body unexpectedly. I would feel my throat clench as if fingers wrapped around me. I never knew where the fear was going to show up next. I would finally succumb to the body aches, pains, and feelings. I found myself lying on the ground a lot.

The ground, the earth, was my safe haven during this Season of my life transition.

My head would spin me dizzy, my heart would be shattered, and I would do anything to make the pain a lesson. I wanted off of this spinning ride. The steadiness of the ground became my therapy. I lay on the floor of my closet. I lay on the carpet in my bedroom. I mainly lay on the floor in the home office that I claimed as my sacred space. I would also lay on the ground outside, even if it was snowy and cold. I was grounding myself down from the emotional rollercoaster. I held myself steady with all of the grounding techniques I could muster.

When you hear stories of people hitting their bottom or lowest part of their journey, they often start with, "I was laying on the bathroom floor in tears." Being held by Mother Earth is one of the most incredible ways to heal our emotions – at least that's what I've experienced. We all have Root Chakra energy, and the ability to connect to the earth and heal ourselves is a beautiful place to start.

PAINS OF THE HEART: HEARTBREAK, HEARTACHE, AND BETRAYAL

I do not feel I am an expert on heart pain. My own experiences cannot meet or completely encapsulate the explanation of pain in the heart space. I have lived through heartbreak, heartache, and betrayal. However, there are so many different experiences around these various pains. I count my blessings that I have lived with a limited understanding of heart pain. I would never wish this type of suffering on any person. I can only speak to the direct experiences I have felt around the sensations of heartache and heartbreak.

As humans, we all likely have experienced the sensation of *heartache*. As children, we may feel sorrow for all kinds of reasons, and we are typically encouraged to wipe our tears and move on or get over it. Disappointments can vary, but sadness is usually a byproduct of disappointment and can cause heartache. Heartache and disappointment can be felt in our bodies. Sometimes, we can feel other people's heartache and disappointment too. When I see other people in my life have moments of sadness caused by heartache, I can feel their sadness, even if there is no direct correlation to me.

Empathy for others can also cause suffering or pain in our hearts. Seeing others in distress can trigger sensations of heartache. These reactions can be felt in our bodies when we watch a sad movie or witness the horrors of the nightly news. The devastation of lives from floods, fires, wars, or even the loss of income or job security. We may notice that we feel heartbreak for others; that is a collective pain. For those of us who are empathetic to others' experiences, we have to be careful about how we manage or allow the pain of others to make an impact on our daily lives.

Then we can also feel *heartbreak* sensations that can feel like the entire heart cavity has shattered into pieces. It can be hard to breathe. Heartbreak can be a terrifying place to be, causing so much pain and sadness that the body and mind can shut down from the trauma of the pain.

I believe the first real heartbreak sensation I experienced was the pain I felt during a series of break-ups with my long-time boyfriend throughout high school. Starting from my sophomore year through my senior year of high school, I became aware of the sensation of pain in the body caused by emotions. I remember downplaying the significance of the situation in my mind, but the actual pain was hot, intense, and drove me to make some poor decisions. As a young Maiden, I believed that my heartache was the worst pain in the world. Of course, I can now say it wasn't the worst, but it felt like that to me at the time.

After my parent's divorce, I lived mainly with my mother. We moved out of the family home and into a condominium where I would witness my mother's pain and heartbreak each morning as she would scramble up eggs for breakfast and prepare for work. You can see the pain of heartbreak on the faces of humans. I would continue my daily life as a freshman as if nothing was wrong, as if I wasn't witnessing my mother's pain.

In the evenings, I would lay on my bed in my room, knocking out homework or talking on the phone with friends, and I would watch my mother out the window as she walked out her pain. She would put on her headphones and walk circles around the condo complex nightly. She walked through the pain of her divorce. She walked through her heartache, and slowly over time, the scrambled eggs were less watery with tears. She made an imprint on me that we can move pain through the body.

Another type of heart pain can also be felt when a person may wrong another person. When someone violates your trust, we refer to it as betrayal. At some point in our lives, we likely have all experienced betrayal to some degree. Either we have been the person to betray someone, or we have felt betrayed, especially by those we love. This is a harrowing experience, and the heart pain is excruciating.

The betrayal I imposed on my ex-husband and my family to a degree was undoubtedly a painful, heartwrenching experience. Yet, not having set out to hurt anyone, I still have to sit in the seat as a person who betrayed another. It will always be a part of me and my story. A story I have replayed hundreds of times in my mind. I carry this on my sleeve like the *Scarlet Letter,* the letter "A" as a reminder to me that our paths are not always laid out perfectly.

I had no choice but to stand through the pains of judgment for my betrayal so that I might create a better life for myself. All the lessons I have learned through that process were invaluable to me. Perhaps Nathaniel Hawthorn also had intentions that the letters we wear on our sleeves are the grades we earn in our lessons through life.

GRIEF: THE MIRROR OF LOVE

My dear friend once told me that grief can quietly come in and land on your heart softly and gently and out of nowhere, even as you are strumming along in your day-to-day moments. Grief can feel sweet and tender with memories of the loss, and on the other hand, it can feel like you're wearing a thick wool blanket that has been submerged into water and without a proper ring out.

The feelings and sensations of grief come in many disguises.

Many great psychologists have studied grief, and the conclusion seems to be that it is a non-linear cycle. One in which you feel you may go through all the phases of grief that Dr. Elisabeth Kubler-Ross brilliantly describes in the theory of the Grief Cycle. Still, ultimately you may feel a wide variety of emotions when you experience grief.

According to Kubler-Ross, phases of grief can circle back and spiral and bounce around from any of the following set of emotions.

Kubler-Ross Grief Cycle

- Denial: Avoidance, Confusion, Elation, Shock, Fear

- Anger: Frustration, Irritation, Anxiety

- Depression: Overwhelmed, Helplessness, Hostility, Flight

- Bargaining: Struggling to find meaning, Reaching out to others, Telling one's story

Acceptance: Imploring option, New plan in place, Moving on

When you know and understand grief, then you know and understand love. I have found the dark side of love is grief, and I have become its constant companion.

I have held lots of space for my grief through this Season, and suffering has held me too. When we can identify our emotions and know when we feel the sensation of grief, we can know or understand that love is the other side of our suffering. For me, finding time to be in tune with my emotions created what we refer to as a Self-Care practice. When I sat with myself in my discomfort, pain, grief, or even my joy, contentment, and happiness, that is when I could create a Self-Care practice to meet all the needs of my emotions. From my experience, being in tune with your own heart and having a solid Self-Love practice, you can also be very clear and compassionate when your heart needs care through the grief process.

The actions and behaviors that can come from grief need to be approached with compassion and understanding. You are worthy of love, forgiveness, and kindness from others, even if you lash out in anger or feel helpless and depressed from grief. All people would be more open and honest about processing emotions in my dream world. Additionally, we would have more empathy and understanding toward one another. It could soften our interactions if we knew what each person was experiencing emotionally at that moment.

Once I grasped that concept of trying to better understand where someone may be emotionally, it helped me recognize how I could process my own emotions. I could be sweeter and more forgiving to myself; it opened my eyes to how other people's actions, words, and behaviors were also just their expression of grief and not to take it personally. This is still a practice for me.

I often have to remind myself that my grief has the opportunity to turn into a beautiful gift in the coming seasons. That grief is never a process that has a completion. That I can recognize the grief in my body and in my heart. I can allow it to be without judgment. I honor the gifts that my grief has taught me, and I know that I will be able to sit with the suffering of those I love dearly.

GROUNDING INTO SANCTUARY OF SELF

We can all agree that humans need a connection to each other, and in my belief, we all need a connection to another source. For many people, their relationship with their pets can bring all the comforts, love, support, and purpose they require. For others, there is a need to have a deep connection with other people in profound ways. As we all traverse through this life journey, it is imperative to know what your intrinsic needs are for healthy relationships. From my perspective of learning and growth, it all has to start with your connection to Self.

Using the Root Chakra's energy to ground you into your authentic essence and inner knowing will create unlimited opportunities to find healthy connections to others throughout your life. Knowing your true Self will guide you through the path of education, your career, building your network of friends and allies, building and growing a family, and most crucial, your sense of Self to build healthy partnerships with others.

As every human being has different interests, pursuits, tastes, and exposure, I don't know if I could speak to all the ways others can find their sense of Self. However, I will say my experience and understanding have come in my moments of solitude. I learn the most when I have space to be alone and quiet with my thoughts, emotions, and sensations. Listening to my inner thoughts has not always been a pleasant experience either.

I reflect on many chapters of my life where my internal dialogue was cruel, unkind, and fiercely hard on my poor Soul (and body). It takes conscious effort to combat the "itty bitty shitty committee" that many have referenced. However, being alone with my Self has been the best way to root and ground into my inner thoughts. And, as hard as I can be on my Self, I have found so much sweetness and softness within me.

In this Winter Season, there have been moments when I have had to tease out the difference between loneliness and healthy solitude. There were moments of being alone when I found my "committee" of inner thoughts incredibly hurtful and destructive. The self-loathing and shaming that I was capable of dishing out to myself was pretty radical. Listening to my inner thoughts and dialogue was unbearable to hear at times. I knew I had hurt a person I cared for deeply, and I intuitively knew that this person and I would eventually not care for each other the same way. If I turned my back on myself, or shamed myself to death, figuratively and perhaps physically, that would eventually just cause more harm to my children.

I knew I had to dig really hard through the waters of grief to get past my own inner critic. The sadness and depression solidified in my heart. Every day felt like a battle in which I would find a way to bypass the awful things I heard to survive. Each morning I would wake up and seek refuge from the haunting words. Alone, either in my comfy green chair or the home office that had transformed into my sacred space, I would tuck myself in tightly to avoid the destruction.

I filled my head-space with guided meditations, podcasts on personal and spiritual growth, or audiobooks. And over time, I continued to find ways to lessen the hurtful words I would hear from my "committee." In time, I found the courage to instead listen to my inner guides for thoughts and wisdom, which ultimately ended the war.

The ability to build a safe sanctuary within my own mind and heart became my fortress. I continued to build up walls of self-knowing so that I, too, couldn't take myself down. I was also up against significant people in my life trying to take me down, and my Sanctuary of Self is what kept me alive. Over time my solitude became my homeland.

MY FAVORITE WAYS TO GROUND INTO THE SANCTUARY OF SELF

Knowing who you are at the root or core of your inner Being is imperative to navigating this experience we are all having on planet Earth at this time. I would encourage you to find a moment alone to list out how you connect with your Self. List all the ways. Then find some time each week to create moments of Connection to Self. If this is all new and seems unrealistic to do in a busy life and schedule, I challenge you to get creative on making the time for yourself. Start with small, incremental steps. You will be so grateful once you make the time, and all the fantastic other humans in your life will appreciate you more, for when they see you permitting yourself to connect, they hopefully will find the time and space to do the same for themselves.

Being able to find the space to ground into your inner sanctuary will be the place in which you can return again and again: open, available, and safe. Make time for yourself. Make space to learn and love your Self. Create a beautiful new sanctuary.

Root Chakra Grounding

A slow walk around the yard: Earthing and Grounding.

Sacral Chakra Grounding

Dancing: Shake your booty by yourself while you get ready in your bathroom or if you have alone moments in your kitchen. Turn up your favorite playlist and dance! If you can find a local group that supports a safe environment for free expression, those are my favorite. One of my dearest friends hosts Shakti Shakedowns, where the music moves everyone in a free, Spirit-lead fashion of dance and movement.

Solar Plexus Chakra Grounding

Hiking: Even if I'm hiking with my partner, we find silence between us so that we can connect with our inner Self and with Mother Nature. A quick-paced run on the beautifully paved Heart of Ohio Trail or any nature run is always enjoyable.

Heart Chakra Grounding

Cooking: I have always thought I was a terrible cook, or at least that was what I had learned to believe about myself. However, once I moved into my own house and was responsible for cooking for myself and the kids fully, I found so much joy and connection in being in the kitchen alone, listening to music, making a mess, and putting so much love into my meal. Thank you, Hello Fresh, for the few months of subscription that made this way easier and possible.

Throat Chakra Grounding

Yoga: on my mat with music, people, heart-led instruction, all pure bliss, sitting knee to knee with one or several of my Sisters to process what my Soul and heart need to speak.

Third Eye Chakra Grounding

Self Care: These moments could include soaking in a hot Epsom salt bath, hot tea, and journal, stretching my body in silence, playing Florence and the Machine while I take a hot shower, and getting "cuted-up," which includes a little make-up, and blowout of my hair.

Driving: Oh, my car is my sanctuary! Podcasts with Brene Brown, Playlists on Spotify, or just maximizing the moments of silence.

Crown Chakra Grounding

Connection to our High Sources, our Divine Energy, God, Goddess, and our ancestors and angels can allow the expansiveness of our Crown Chakra energy. In turn, this leads to a grounded sensation.

- Sitting in my Sanctuary space - quiet, alone
- Slow walks in nature, without any technology to capture the moment
- A morning or evening meditation practice
- Yin and Restorative yoga

Sacral Chakra: Lessons on the Journey

My Maiden whispers to Me: *"Well, look at you!"*

Me: *"I'm enjoying the warmth of the sun on my skin. These first few days of warmth before Spring really begins are the best here in Ohio."*

My Maiden: *"I don't know; you just look so different. I keep reading all the memes on Instagram about people adding weight in this Global Pandemic, or shut-down and quarantine - what they call the 'Quarantine-Fifteen.' But you! You look like you lost weight in your body. It feels familiar to when I was in my prime years as a Maiden in your body."*

Me: *"Yeah, well, it's also called stress, missy, I don't think I would choose the stress of what I have gone through this Winter as a healthy means to losing weight. But yeah, I also have more time in my life to walk in nature and do a quick morning workout each day. Not having to leave the house to get kids to school and to get to my office each day has been truly a gift of time for me."*

My Maiden: *"Well I can feel your sacral energy is a flowing Sister! I can feel you are freeing up your heart space with lots of love for yourself which is helping to keep that sacral energy flowing too!"*

Me: *"Yeah, you know, I do feel like I am feeling more grounded and confident in my Self. I do feel stronger in my body, and that of course, is making me feel more sexy and powerful, you're right!"*

My Maiden: *"This is good! This is really good! Please for me, let's use this sacral energy to keep going. Spring Equinox is around the corner. This is my favorite time of year. The official kick-off to Spring Season, which is truly the inauguration of Maiden Season (ahem!).*"

Me: "*Yes, I know, sweet girl. Don't you worry! I will find a beautiful way to honor the Maiden Spirit. I love having my daughter help me create an altar for the Spring Equinox and to celebrate the creativity around new beginnings. I'm sure in these quarantine days, I will find ways to honor you, and for sure new beginnings for me.*"

My Maiden: "*Oh good! Okay, creative art and play, dancing and feeling sexy. You need more of that in your life right now. Maybe you can mess around with making a TicTok video with the kids or something?*"

Me: (laughing) "*Okay, okay, let's not get out of control here Maiden!*"

My Maiden: "*Oh come on Kerry! I think it would be great for you. Just have some fun, and bring more light into your life. You are coming out of the darkness, and sometimes you have to just create your own light to shine.*"

SANCTUARY OF SOUL

The light so bright, a glow of gold and pink

Warmed by the embers of flame

A beacon of illumination

The softness and care

Sweetened by the dew

Gentle for all to feel

The strength and determination

Like the Phoenix rising

Resilience again and again

The freedom of truth

The words to be shared

Bravery for all to witness

The beauty of acceptance

Creation of a universal love

The eternal embrace

The knowing of Self

True love everlasting

The Sanctuary of the Soul

MY HO'OPONOPONO PRAYER

To my Mother, my Father, my Brother. To my Sisters far and wide. To my Children. To my Grandmothers, and their Grandmothers, and their Grandmothers. To my Uncles. To my Aunties. To my Cousins. To my Husband. To his Family. To All of our Friends. To those that may know of me and those that yet don't. I say these words to you ...

I am sorry.

I wake up each morning knowing I have another day of life to live. I wake up and begin my pursuit of forgiveness each morning just as consistently as the sun rolls up the horizon. I start with my Children. I am sorry for creating such a disturbance in your life. I am sorry for the destruction of routine, of security, of knowing that your life as you knew it has changed. I'm sorry to my family for breaking the traditions. I'm sorry to my once husband. After eighteen years of marriage, I'm sorry for breaking your heart and shattering your pride. To his family, I'm sorry. The explanations will likely not make their way to you, and I am incredibly sorry for this. I'm sorry to the friends who no longer speak to me, and I am sorry to friends that have shown up to support me every day with love and compassion in their hearts. I am sorry for the perception of a perfect marriage that has been destroyed. I am sorry for the 'happily ever after' and the idealism of perfect love. I am so sorry.

I am sorry.

Please forgive me.

Thank you.

I love you.

Please forgive me.

Please forgive me for betraying a relationship that I held sacred for many years. Please forgive me for not being honest and truthful. Please forgive me for creating heartache, heartbreak, and shatter. Please forgive me for following the path less traveled and being brave enough to ask big questions. Please forgive me for not allowing complacency. Forgive me for searching and seeking a more authentic sense of Self and listening to the whispers of my Soul. Please, forgive me.

I am sorry.

Please forgive me.

Thank you.

I love you.

Thank you.

Thank you to those who have witnessed the cracking open and the essence of BEING that comes seeping through those cracks. Thank you to my children, who have continued to LOVE and adapt to the new ways, routines, rules, and lifestyle. Thank you to my extensive group of wolf women. The women who have shown up, listened, hugged, witnessed my tears, danced with me by the fire, and held my hand as I walked right through it. I have felt your hands on my back for years, and when I wobble, stumble and fall, your hands and hearts pick me back up. Thank you.

I am sorry.

Please forgive me.

Thank you.

I love you.

I love you.

I Am Love.

I LOVE.

I love the depth of love that shows up every day. I love knowing that love is love. I love the sensation of love from the top of my head right down to my toes. I love the embrace. I love the soft and sweet. The strength that comes through and the deep knowing that LOVE WINS every time. The pandemic of hatred is growing deeper in our culture, and I know that right now is the scariest and most important time to stand in the depths of LOVE. So if it feels like the House of Cards is crumbling around you, just look for the Queen of Hearts, pick her up and start to rebuild your house again. I love you.

I am sorry.

Please forgive me.

Thank you.

I love you.

I seek this Ho'oponopono Prayer daily, moment to moment, like a mantra, repeating it for hours in my head or just a few minutes. It always finishes with these words:

Kerry Hope,

I am sorry.

Please forgive me.

Thank you.

I love you.

I'm Sorry. Please Forgive Me. Thank You. I Love You.

Kerry Hope

FORGIVENESS OF SELF: INTROSPECTION AND SELF-AWARENESS

There are so many great quotes about forgiveness. One of my favorite messages is:

"You'll never know how strong your heart is until you learn to forgive the person that broke it."

- Anonymous

The righteous act of forgiving and the ability to forgive someone who hurt you can take so much courage. All the great thought leaders would agree in the end. You always walk away with Freedom. I understand why it's hard for people to forgive another. The pain and harm that others can place on another can be unfathomable for me to understand and accept. However, the power one gives to the hurt, or the power you give to the person or people that did the wrongdoing, is not worth the amount of pain that continues to be held in your body.

Freedom. Allowing forgiveness gives you freedom but doesn't take away the "wrong" from the other person.

When I look back on the different chapters, seasons, and events in my life, I can see how easy it is to forgive. The power I gain from forgiveness, in turn, gives me a greater ability to love. On the other hand, I can see human error, and I have also been very grateful that my life path has not led me to experience severe pain brought on by another person.

However, I do know pain from loss. I can sit in the empathy chair with my friends who have lost a child to cancer or other unforeseen death and attempt to feel into their pain. Although, as a parent, I have said, "The pain I feel when I imagine the loss of a child is simply unbearable." I understand that I may never know how to forgive that sorrow. I am not here to give advice or judge anyone's experience around forgiveness and loss. I am simply here to sit alongside your pain.

The forgiveness of other people takes courage. It does open a new level of freedom for your Soul, and it will show you how to love in a more significant, more profound way. Learning to forgive yourself is also one of the most courageous acts you can make. Humans make errors. Really good people can hurt other really good people. There is no escaping making mistakes in our lives.

Often our acts of hurting others happen when we only look out for our own best interests. We can cause pain and harm to people we love, and really it is not about the other person; it is about ourselves.

When I went through the fire of acknowledging the betrayal to my husband, I thought there was no way in hell I would ever forgive myself. I had plotted how the shame would look and feel inflicted on me for the years to come. What punishments did I deserve? How would it feel to be unforgiven by my family? I don't know the exact moment when my mindset shifted on this, but eventually, my Soul self came through. The wisdom came to me from all three of my archetypes, in different wording, of course, but ultimately the Mother's words spoke the loudest to me. Here is what she said to me in my courageous act of forgiving Myself.

My Mother Self whispers to me:

"Screw them. If they are not going to forgive you, then you have to forgive yourself. You are only following what your truest Soul Self is asking of you. You are allowing your own life to be lived in a way that is true to who you are as a person and being your best version of yourself. If they cannot forgive you for the path you took to get in alignment with your Self, then your freedom will lie in your own forgiveness."

If there is any significant action that I would deem courageous, it is the righteous act of forgiving myself. Likely some people will never be able to forgive me for the changes I have made in my life. However, many of my family and friends have found happiness for me in their hearts, and I can presume they have gained freedom and love. The others will perhaps be shackled to the anger or hatred they have for me leaving my marriage, and that is on them. That is their choice to lack the exchange of love and freedom. I can't control how they choose to heal. All I know is that my choice to forgive myself has led me to a life with a beautiful, deeply loving new partner—a healthier way of living free from codependency, alcoholism, manipulation, and control.

I think the courage I made to forgive myself is worth it. I am worth it. This life is mine to live, and if I let shame run my life, I will be a prisoner to others. In addition, my act of forgiving myself is now teaching my kids that they, too, will make mistakes. If they can learn to accept their wrong-doings, speak the words of a genuine apology, and then learn to let it go for themselves, they too will live more vital, more freeing, and more loving lives.

CONNECTING TO YOUR CRONE WISDOM: VISUALIZATION

Before you read this next section, please find yourself in a place of peace and solitude. Have a journal and pen nearby (or use this book to jot down any notes) so that you may capture any wisdom you gain as you connect to your inner knowing from your Mother and Crone archetypes.

Pause now to close your eyes, and take three slow, deep, long, rich breaths in and out.

As you settle into yourself, begin by noticing all your sensations around your body. What does your clothing feel like on your skin? Are you warm, or is there a chill in the air? What smells do you notice around you? How does this book feel in your hands or on your lap? Step yourself through all five senses of your Being.

How, at this moment, are you caring for your personal needs? Adjust yourself accordingly, and provide any additional comforts for yourself. Are your toes covered with cozy socks or a blanket? Do your shoulders feel wrapped up and secure? Or do you need a gentle breeze of a fan to keep you cool?

As you settle in, take a moment to welcome the elder, wise Crone that resides within you. You may notice a lightness to your Being or an overwhelming sense of calm and softness.

It's a cold, snowy day outside, and you decide to climb out of your cozy nest of blankets to begin the layering process of thermals and warm pants, sweater, jacket, scarf, hat, gloves, and boots. The outdoors is calling for you to take a walkabout and feel the remaining sunlight bless the natural landscape before setting.

As you begin your journey through the snow-covered woodland path, you can see a flash of red from a cardinal flying through the trees and brush just ahead of your steps. You notice how this particular bird is not only looking for his mate but seems to be heading down the same path in which you are headed too.

As you step one boot in front of the other, you are paying attention to the sound of the crunching snow when you start to notice a tiny little wood cabin just ahead on the path. The glow of the yellow lights shines out of the cabin, and fireplace smoke releases from the chimney, giving you an overwhelming sense of comfort and warmth. Just as you are approaching the cabin, the cardinal decides to make a quick stop at the bird feeder sitting outside the cabin window. The bird's movement must have caught the eye of the cabin resident as they slowly open up the door to catch a better view of the bird as it feeds.

Your presence, too, catches the attention of an elder, grey-haired woman. And as you get closer, you notice that she carries her body and facial features very similar to you. You have an overwhelming sense of excitement as she is waving to you and offering for you to come inside her sweet, warm, and inviting home. The aroma is so pleasing to your senses that you continue to find your way inside graciously.

The woman invites you to join her for a cup of tea, the water kettle already whistling and two mugs with tea bags ready to go. She has been waiting for your arrival. You feel welcomed and sit down at her kitchen table to steep your tea.

The beautiful woman across the table from you has a glimmer in her eyes and a soft smile that frames her entire face. Crone Speaks: *"I am so grateful you ventured out to find me. My day is better for your visit. Thank you for stopping by."*

Your hands find their way to your heart, one covering the other, and you reflect back to her a sweet and endearing smile back. *"Dearest Crone, thank you for being supportive to me, and thank you for all your insights. Please tell me, what is it that I need to hear from you today?"*

You Listen.

What wisdom does your inner Crone want you to know?

How can she provide you with insight into a particular situation you have in your life?

You take a moment to reflect on her wisdom, her years of experience, what she has endured, and how she came through it all. What else does she say?

At this time, she slowly pushes back from the table and stands up. She softly moves to another room in the cabin, only to return quickly with an object in her hands. The Crone reaches over to you and offers you this item. What does your Crone want you to have?

You thank your dear Crone for the gift. You gently reach for this item and know this is precisely what you need. What is it? What do you need to help you in this Season of Life?

We always receive what we need in the most perfect times of our lives. What might this item bring for you? How might this thing help you? Be grateful for whatever comes to your mind and heart.

As you feel you have gained the perfect advice and wisdom from your wise, elder Self, you begin to gather your layers and put back on your boots. Your heart is full of so much gratitude for you feel as if you are walking away with such a unique treasure. You thank your Crone again for the lovely time and tea as you turn to leave. *"I will be back again soon,"* you say.

As you are walking back down the trail on which you came, you reflect on the great wisdom of your heart. As you continue on this path, you know that you are wiser and stronger with this inner knowing. So you smile and walk peacefully before the final dusk sets.

The wisdom of your inner Crone is with you always. You can always grab a hot tea and sit with the warmth of your own inner wisdom at any time.

III

THE SEASON OF SPRING

HONORING YOUR HEALING

And just like that, we all begin again.

The coming of Spring each year is our reminder that new beginnings are required. All the life that slept dormant will awaken again. The natural world begins to stretch into fresh, new shoots of life, and the brown grasses start to shimmer into a lighter, pale green. The rebirth is inevitable. Spring is when we realize that we need to stretch and shoot into new colors of being. After all, we are part of the natural world.

When we initiate a healing process for our Souls, we might have to accept that there is no completion to the process. We want our healing cycles to have a beginning and an end in our perfect worlds. If we can find the best tools and ways to heal our wounds, the start and end of each healing cycle will look different, similar to the natural world. The tree trunks grow mightier every Spring Season, even if a buck used it to sharpen his antlers. The leaves may shift shape and size from saplings into full-grown trees regardless of sunlight exposure. We can find the mile-markers in our everyday situations when we step back and take a broader view of any progress made throughout the healing journey.

Springtime seems to invoke excitement in the natural world. There is also a sense of excitement when initiating a new beginning. How can you mirror the wild world of the Spring Season with the anticipation and shoots of blooms in your daily life? Can you allow the same sensation to seep into the new possibilities of honoring a healing journey for yourself? Celebrating even the slightest movements you make toward a healing journey will eventually bring beautiful fresh life blooms.

Letter to Crone, March 2020

My Dearest Crone,

The time of transition has come for us all. As we bid farewell to Winter's cold, damp days, we begin to see and feel the evolution of new life this Spring. However, this Spring feels very different from before, as the reality of our global pandemic has reached a heightened state for all of us.

The blessing of having a statewide shut-down is that it has provided beautiful outdoor fun and playful moments. However, in addition to our day-to-day fun, there is also alcohol. Oh, the sweetness of a buzz on a sunny, Spring afternoon. Kids outside shooting hoops and jumping on the trampoline. Roller Skating and Hula-Hooping. Chalk art and tossing footballs. Our afternoons and evenings feel like a fantasy of being together as a family.

However, once we cross the threshold of what we consider a respectable time to have a drink, we do. Martinis. Lots of vodka martinis. Spotify music playing, the warmth of the setting sun, and the perfect cocktail to numb the inevitable pain that finds me in the dark hours.

I feel held captive in a home and a marriage I didn't want to be in anymore. So I look for any cracks in the corners that might allow me to escape. And I found a way in the form of a bottle of Tito's, which moves to a late-night bourbon, which leads to uncomfortable conversations, jackal voices and arguing, passing out in my daughter's room, and avoiding intimacy as if it was COVID-19.

I am in the depths of my heartbreak and loss. I am sitting in the unknown about the security of my marriage. I am anguishing over what has transpired for this incredible woman within her life since I am no longer in communication with her. I have fallen madly in love with this person and miss her so much.

I am weak. I am scared. I do not know if I can heal the heartache that I am feeling every moment of every day. Am I going to lose everything? Am I going to lose my kids? Am I going to lose my dignity?

Please, dearest Crone, give me your insights of hope. I need to know that the world is not ending and that I will get to the other side of this pandemic and marital crisis. So please send me a message that I will be okay.

In all respects and love,

Kerry Hope

Sacral Chakra: Lessons on the Journey

My Maiden whispers to Me: *"Hey you, it's me again."*

Me: *"Oh hello."*

My Maiden: *"I see you are in a pretty low place these days. I also see you trying your hardest to make something work that isn't working anymore."*

Me: *"Well, yeah, I am clearly in an incredibly uncomfortable situation."*

My Maiden: *"I mean, you're trying so hard to accept something that isn't acceptable. You know how I know?"*

Me: *"Oh, please enlighten me, my dear!"*

My Maiden: *"I can see it on your face when you are being intimate in your marriage."*

Me: *"Really? My face, huh?"*

My Maiden: *"Well, that and your body is in pain. You know that the discomfort of sex is not normal right?"*

Me: *"Oh my gosh!! I am NOT having a sex talk with my younger version of Self!"*

My Maiden: *"Yep! Let's talk. I can't sit back and not speak up when I see that sacral energy blocked, and in turn, it is causing you some deep pain, right?"*

Me: *"I mean, I think it's normal. I'm in a challenging place in my life and trying to figure out all these factors of who I am, who I am as a mother, daughter, friend, lover, and how to live the life that I have created, so yeah, I'm sure my body is having some repercussions through all of this transition."*

My Maiden: *"Hey, I get it. I am here for you, trust me. If you can work on unblocking this Sacral energy, I think everything will become clearer to you. You will be able to look at every situation a little more clearly and differently."*

Me: *"Yeah, that all makes sense. Sacral Chakra is the source of creativity and sexuality, and pleasure. I feel I am undeserving of feeling good, pleasure, or sexy after all that I have been through this Winter."*

My Maiden: *"What?? That is crazy talk!! If your Sacral energy is blocked, you are not truly honoring your entire body's system. You need to spend a little time focusing on that sacral energy, my dear, that will set you free."*

Me: *"So what do I do if I can't express myself freely while being intimate?"*

My Maiden: *"Well, let's get creative! You can still open your energy through dancing. You can always wear clothing that makes you feel sexy. Notice your body posturing. Sit like a sex goddess, walk as if you are a Queen, and sip your tea with your arm raised a tiny bit, so you feel empowered. You can create sexuality in your body without having sex. Oh! And when you get a warm day this Spring, sneak out to the backyard and sit topless to feel the sun's warmth."*

Me: *"Ohh, yeah, that does sound amazing. I hear you, sweet Maiden. You are right, and my blocked sacral has been causing a lot of pain. I need to also work on my Throat Chakra and speak up about these pains and blocks?"*

My Maiden: *"Oh yes, please! Speak Up! Play, Dance, Act Sexy, Be Sexy. Create art. You can do this!"*

SEEDS OF POSSIBILITY

I walk the earth slowly. I can feel the damp, cold under my feet. The electromagnetic energy surges through the bottom of my feet. Heal, then middle foot, then toes. Again. I repeat with my other foot. The ground is soft, but the grass is rough, prickly, and brown. The temperature is inviting warmth, but it's not quite ready yet. I am walking on unsteady ground and contemplating the new beginning that is taking place all around me. I wrap my shawl around my arms tighter, holding myself tighter. I take a few deeper breaths. Wet nature surrounds me, and its scent pours into my lungs.

I found a spot, a down tree resting on the ground since fall. Beautiful, old, and majestic even as she laid still and silent. I felt the urge to climb onto the tree's large trunk and rest. As I sat at this moment, I knew that I was doing the best I could for myself. I knew I had the means, tools, and knowledge to help myself heal, yet I knew I would receive guidance and confirmation from my Spirit guides, angels, and Divine when I needed it. My heart could feel the reassurance that I needed to feel at this moment.

Looking down beneath the trunk of this enormous tree, under the dormant brush and wet, decaying leaves, was a teeny, tiny sprout from a little, tiny seed. I smiled and noticed.

Look! That little sprout found a way through the damp, cold, heavy earth's muck through the decaying weight of the leaves and brush. She used the stored energy she was building all Winter long, and she creatively found a way through.

There! I exclaimed. If that teeny-tiny seed found the strength and a creative way to work through the situation, I know I can too.

I finished my hike that afternoon and found a way to create a beautiful new ritual that a friend had suggested. First, I collected some dirt, rocks, twigs, and leaves from my yard, placing all items in a large glass jar. Next, I added a few crystals that would bring protection to my ritual. Finally, I added a photo of myself. I had taken a simple selfie in the woods and printed it off at a kiosk while picking up groceries. I put all the items together, and then I said this prayer:

The seed in me will use my strength and energy to find a way to sprout into a new version of me. I will continue to heal my heart and all the hearts around me with my love and passion for truth and acceptance. This seed will grow no matter the aversions I may face. And so it is!

I then proceeded to fill the large jar with water to activate the growth. Finally, I tied a memorable piece of weaving I acquired when traveling in Peru around the jar's lid, and I sat it on my altar where the Eastern sunlight would drench it each morning with light.

For the few months of this final phase of my transition, I would see the photo of me floating in the water and looking more prominent than usual due to the contour of the jar. I saw this amazing woman looking back at me with passion in her eyes and the warrior in her Spirit.

And then, one day, after spending time in my sacred space pulling oracle cards and doing morning meditation, I looked up to the jar, and there it was, a teeny-tiny sprout of hope that came through. *I am going to be okay.* I then emptied the contents of the jar. I laid the photo in the sun to dry and then burned it to release all she had endured in her activation and ritual. And so it was!

THE DISMANTLING OF A MARRIAGE

From 2002 to 2020 marks the years, the days and the moments shared in our marriage.

Sacred memories of our ceremony and celebrations with our friends and family at the French Lick Resort in beautiful Southern Indiana.

In this time, we shared the most incredible highs, built a beautiful home, traveled and journeyed, supported each other through our work careers, and 'peopled' two great dogs. But, our biggest, most incredible win has been our two exceptional children.

We have had the most spectacular moments with our two kids from conception to nine and eleven years old. The love, the laughter, the tears, and the heartbreak we have shared have carried us through our marriage; I will never forget this.

As a collective society, we are all faced with the trials of figuring out a new way of living and working through a global pandemic. I have an additional task: working through the dismantling of a marriage.

We will meet the difficulties of reconfiguring a new way of living as co-parents and partners. We will detangle and unwind from the lives we have shared for almost twenty years. We continue to emphasize the love and support of our beautiful children. Although we have dismantled our marriage, I will always love and care for my once husband and continue to honor our contract as co-parents.

HEALING THE INNER CHILD

As I attempt to save a marriage at the heart of the pandemic and the global shut down—the threat of losing meaningful relationships and the consequence of losing my children is traumatic to my Soul. I desperately was trying to comfort my Inner Child along the way.

My little Inner Child was scared. So this sweet darling would hunt me down in the dead of night and crawl into bed with me to snuggle, or she would find me laying in the corner of my closet in tears, *"I know you're sad, hurt, and scared, but so am I,"* this little voice would say to me.

"Are we going to be okay?" I felt her sadness, and it often overpowered my adult despair. So here is what I would say to my sweet little Inner Child:

"Yes, my darling sweetheart, we will be just fine. And you know what? We will be even better than fine. I'm scared, too. I have many feelings that I haven't ever felt before, and sometimes that can be super scary. And right now, I don't know what to do and I feel terrified, so what would be great is if we could just have some fun and play together. That would help me not feel so scared. So can we just have some fun and play?"

I spent every day finding a way to play. My sweet Inner Child was blessed to have one of the most epic, creative, fun-loving, and spirited playmates in the universe right there beside me in the form of my daughter. My sweet, loving nine-year-old, live-in playmate was thrilled to have a good last run being a little girl in this chapter of her life. I knew that this was divine timing. I knew that childhood play with my daughter was the best form of therapy and medicine I could have. I knew time was waning for my marriage, and playing with my daughter was the perfect distraction for me in this Season of my life.

Letter to Inner Child, April 2020

To my darling sweetheart,

I am here. I am here for you, and I love you so much.

Thank you, sweet girl, for being willing to let me love and nurture you throughout your life.

We have shared such special moments. You have made me smile in joy, and I am honored to be able to hold you in all your sadness too. You are a beautiful little girl. Witty and so funny. I know you love to talk, and I love to listen to all your words and thoughts.

I love creating art with you, as we were on our knees creating a loving, healing art piece dedicated to our earth and all who are suffering from COVID-19. We even included the solar system and planets and drew our family's astrological constellations. I know you loved that so much. We have burned bonfires together, built cup towers, created a mandala in the fairy garden, skipped, swung from the Corner Tree, reaching our toes to the sky, made giant bubbles, and built the most epic fort in the basement. I have loved being in all your energy as a little girl.

You make me so proud. I am incredibly proud of what a magical little girl you are, how happy you make your family, and how sensitive and concerned you are with everyone around you. Thank you. Thank you for making me rollerskate. Thank you for allowing me to love you in all your greatness. Thank you for allowing

me to love you when you are in being yourself, even
though standing in your truth is very hard.

Finally, I just wanted to say that your playmate,
who happens to be my lovely daughter, is an epic
Soul. You, darling sweetheart, are so incredibly
lucky to have such a fantastic friend. You truly are
blessed with this sacred contract.

I love you ALWAYS. And I will love YOU in ALL-WAYS.

Kerry Hope

MAY DAY, MAY DAY

May 2, 2020, the day after Bealtaine (or May Day), I woke up feeling foggy and hungover. It was early in the morning or late at night, depending on how one feels about 2:00 a.m. I felt a presence standing over me as I lay sleeping in my daughter's bed with her. I turned around and could see a familiar man's silhouette and heard his words, "All your things are packed up. You can head out in the morning." I listened to his words, and I knew what he meant, yet I was confused. Why was he up so late, and what did he mean by "my things"? I continued to lay in bed the remaining morning hours, frightened of what I might discover.

When I felt the hour seemed reasonable enough, I crawled out of bed and crept down the stairs so quietly as to not wake the sleeping dragon. Sure enough, there was all my stuff. Everything that I viewed as sacred and vital was boxed up, put in a laundry basket, or just laid out in the front foyer of our house. The little sacred space I used as my healing room for the past several months was emptied to the very last crystal stone.

He's kicking me out. He's kicking me out of my own home, the house we built and created. The home I wobbled through the front entrance with two brand new babies twenty-three months apart. The place I had cared for, decorated, scrubbed, mopped, vacuumed, danced in; all the memories that I created in this house for fifteen years. And I was asked to leave it: the countless celebrations, parties, dinners, and gatherings I hosted and curated. Everything I knew about my home was completely different in the early light of the morning sun, so I did what I knew I could do, I made a cup of coffee.

Ironically, this day had been pre-planned with a couple of Quarantine/outdoor visits from friends. So the day's plan would have been as follows:

10:00 a.m. – nature walk with my friend Courtney.

2:00 p.m. – my best friend Melissa and her two kids would be arriving for an overnight campout in the Airbnb tiny house, and the kids would have their first outdoor play session with their friends since March's mandated statewide shut-down.

5:00 p.m. – One of our closest couple friends would head over for a cook-out and social distance dinner/bonfire.

A perfect set-up for a Spring Saturday after months of lockdown; however, the Universe had a few other things to add to the schedule.

8:00 a.m. – Emergency family meeting to sit down with the kids and tell them that mom is going to move out of the house and that we are going to separate for a little bit and see if that makes mommy or daddy feel any better. Lots of hugs and tears were shared with the kids.

9:00 a.m. – My husband insisted that we head to his parent's house to share the same news. However, they were not privy to the loud voices and arguments the kids had witnessed for several months. We floored them with the information. I watched my dearest mother-in-law weep in her son's arms, and the repetitive word 'disappointing' came from my father-in-law. It was a horrific sight that left me with traumatizing sounds of sadness.

9:30 a.m. – We loaded up my personal items and a few clothes. My daughter helped me move these items into the Ranch rental house with a sweetness in her. I felt like she was an angel from the heavens.

10:00 a.m. – My friend Courtney showed up for a walk. She looked at me and said, *"Let's just take one step at a time, Kerry."* So we walked. I was numb in my body. My eyes were glued wide open. I couldn't blink or cry. I just heard her words.

"What's the next thing you are going to do today?" She asked.

"Iduunknow," I responded.

"Go take a shower," she ordered. *"And then what?"* She asked.

"Idunnknow," I responded.

"You do the next best thing." She continued. *"And after that, you will do the next best thing, and you're going to keep just doing the next best thing all day and all night until the final thing you can do is go to bed. Tomorrow is another day, and you will take another step. You are going to be okay Kerry."*

I took her advice. I showered and prepped food for the cook-out. I went and stared at the boxes that sat in my "new home" that I would need to sort and organize. I couldn't move. I couldn't think. I froze. And I did what Courtney asked me to do, and I did the next best thing over and over, moment by moment.

Shortly after, my closest, dearest friend Melissa pulls into the driveway with her two kids. Her sweet, loving kiddos jump out and instantly start their overnight play sesh with my kids. My beautiful, sad and heartbroken, and confused kids also needed support. So they had two of their favorite playmates show up at the perfect time. They could play outside with friends and be free from the devastation for a few hours. The timing was excellent, and I felt some relief.

Melissa debriefed me on my pains, and while the kids were able to create their imaginative characters for the evening play, she and I went next door to the new house and unpacked. She moved furniture around into new spaces, creating a personal altar space. She cleaned, unpacked, and set up the house so that it would comfort my traumatized and shattered heart for the evening. I couldn't imagine what this day would have been like without Courtney and Melissa showing up for me. They took my hand, picked up each foot, and made it move.

Moment by moment. Step by step. We made it through this life-changing experience that happened all in hours.

Our friends showed up with their BBQ fare and were ready to just hang out at their friend's house as they have always known it to be. Normal. Nothing unusual. We caught up as if everything was unchanged outside of the global pandemic and finally were able to see friends we had not seen in several months. Music. Kids' laughter all around. Bonfire. And all the while, I kept as much of my everyday face as I could muster. I couldn't really feel my face, but I could feel all the energy from my broken husband as we all sat together outside enjoying a beautiful Spring evening, and I could feel his numbness, too.

As the evening came to a close, our friends departed, Melissa and the kids tucked themselves in exhaustion away in the Airbnb. I hugged my kids tightly and kissed their heads goodnight. They headed up to their rooms in fatigue from play and trauma. I gathered up a few additional comforts for the night, and I walked under the moon's light to what would become my healing sanctuary: the cute little house next door to my home that we rented out as an Airbnb. And on this night, there was no arguing, yelling, shaming, and fear. This night, I crawled into a bed not shared by my daughter. I lay in the discomfort of the newness of the environment, listening to the creaks of the house, and then I heard a tiny little voice speaking. It was mine.

"Kerry, get some rest. You did so well today, getting through one step at a time. You are going to either wake up in the morning with severe regret, or you are going to wake up feeling liberated." My eyes closed, and I drifted to sleep. The following day, bright light from the eastern sun warmed my face. I looked around the new surroundings and smiled. Then, the answer came quickly to me.

"Oh, Sweet Liberation."

Music. Coffee. Cleaning and unpacking, and then a tap on my front door. My kids walked down to say good morning and check out the new space. Everything would be alright.

Solar Plexus Chakra: Lessons on the Journey

My Mother whispers to Me: *"Well, look at you!! You had the power to do it this whole time."*

Me: *"I guess I did, huh? I am not sure if what I did was the best decision yet."*

My Mother: *"Stop that nonsense. You DO know! That feeling you have in your abdominal area, that visceral gut feeling of 'fuck yeah!' that you might be feeling right now? That my friend is your solar plexus fully charged and open."*

Me: *"Well, I fell light and liberated, and I have this overwhelming sense of freedom right now. I feel like I can just do whatever I want."*

My Mother: *"Yes!!! You can turn up the music, clean your house, and create a new home, a new life for you and the kids. Utilize your solar plexus energy to keep moving forward positively."*

Me: *"Yes! I can do this, and I feel that I will be okay. I know I have a lot of details to figure out. I know this will not be an easy transition, but I know that I can do this and feel more true to myself than I have felt in a very long time."*

My Mother: *"Oh, good. I am here for you. You've got this and all the backing of power behind you now. Keep just being true to yourself, and everything will work out. I promise."*

REINVENTING SELF

Anyone close to me in my life knows whose music inspires me most. So, of course, some may pause –because this might seem like a trick question– but eventually, they would say, *"Well, Grateful Dead has been her most beloved jam band, but for sure, Madonna is her absolute favorite in terms of inspiration."*

Madonna, for me, has had the leading role of Wild, Authentic Role-modeling since I was a little girl. Some may argue that Madonna may or may not be the best role model for a little girl, but honestly, her journey as an artist always felt perfectly timed to the messaging I needed to hear or feel. I didn't even know what a "virgin" was when I was seven years old, but the song nonetheless shared that she felt good. How great for her!

After all, isn't that what we all want in this life? To feel good?

One of the many things that I have learned from Madonna is her ability to rebuild herself, to reinvent herself. I find her ability to say publicly, this is who I am, and this is what I stand for – over and over – to be awe-inspiring. And more than that, she continues to evolve, find a new version of herself, and keep her talents and career alive well into her sixties.

Over the years, her albums, her music videos, and the six live shows I have seen all point to her enduring legacy. Everything that Madonna stands for has given me permission to make my stance and be my individual person. She has also taught me that I can change and reinvent myself.

When I found myself crawling out of the darkness of my life transition and taking deeper breaths, I realized the sun would still rise and set every day; I was allowed to reinvent my life. The shattered pieces of me that lay strewn across the floor allowed me to see that I could put the pieces of myself and my person together in a whole new way. Although this was incredibly intimidating at first, the first place I started was the grocery store.

I went through aisle by aisle with a general list in mind. I had an utterly barren refrigerator upon moving into my Airbnb rental. I found items in the produce coolers that I had never considered before and bought them. New brands of coffee, loaves of bread, cereals, etc. Everything that I once purchased in my previous life, I found a new item or brand that I would place in my cart.

Even if I looked like a zombie walking through Kroger, this felt exhilarating. I highly recommend this experience to everyone, regardless of whether or not you are recreating a new life for yourself.

Once back in my new house with all the new products, I challenged myself to create new meal options and learn recipes. I found ways to change my daily routine, like drinking lemon water in the morning instead of coffee, finding time to run, and taking nature walks every day. Once businesses started opening back up, I was able to get my hair colored with a new cut. I found myself just wearing a few outfits on rotation. Instead of feeling overwhelmed with options, I kept my life as simple as possible.

Even through the reconstruction process, I was subject to moments of grief, pain, loss, and heartbreak, and I had to be extremely gentle with myself. I was creating space and nurturing myself with love and compassion, all while still having to nurture and care for my children, who were feeling lost, anxious, angry, and sad as well. In addition, I was rebuilding a foundation in a new home, as a single parent, with new rules, new energy, new meals, and a new version of us all. The same us, but in a whole new way of being a family.

Reinventing myself also allows the unknown to be shown and unfolds the mystery. I hope that I can constantly create a newer, better version of myself each Season of my life. I now honor the mystery and stand strong and steady as my person. I know that no matter how I grow and reinvent myself along the way, I will always honor myself as my own home.

"Life is a mystery
Everyone must stand alone
I hear you call my name
And it feels like home."
"Like a Prayer" Madonna

REDEFINING SELF-WORTHINESS

What would it look like if there was a tool to measure your worth? Could it fit into your purse, or is it something you would tuck under your bed at night? If this was an actual item, would your tool of worthiness be glittery and shiny or a solid matte color? It's hard to imagine what a tool like this would look like for most of us because we can't tangibly hold such an object. Yet, daily we find ourselves measuring our worthiness. However, most of us spend our time calculating how much worth we carry in our day-to-day, and we don't even know we are doing it.

Our worthiness can also link to how much love we can receive. My worthiness was the result of how much love I could give. 'Wait though,' you say, 'I can give so much love. To my children, my family, my friends. I give love to all kinds of people in my life.'

Yep, I heard those same thoughts too. And you are not wrong. But, we can give love, even if we may not feel worthy of receiving it back. We can also obtain even more authentic love, love that is more aligned to our truest selves if we know we have the worthiness behind the love we share. If we feel worthy of sharing our love with others, we will feel worthy to receive love from others. It's an 'and both' situation.

Worthiness is lingering behind all the decisions we make each day ourselves. Worthiness is the essence that lives in our throats when we say "no thank you" to the one thing that we know is the one thing we need most. Worthiness consumes the space behind the heart that determines if you make the call, book the appointment, or take the chance to make it happen.

Worthiness directly links to how much love your heart can hold and how much it can give. You may feel overwhelmed with the notion of feeling into your true worth. We can feel overwhelmed in the process of re-establishing our worth to ourselves and also to others. However, for the ability to connect to your heart and connect your unconditional love, you must start with knowing that you are worth it! Knowing that this one single life you are living is worth love. Here is the place I would encourage you to start. Spending time learning who you are will shine the light on your worth and will be a direct connection with your heart.

A lingering family memory has been held amongst my mother, brother, and me for years. When I was in the fourth grade, my mother was doing the parental nightly check-in, standing in the hallway outside our rooms. After confirming our teeth were brushed and the lights were off, she then proceeded to say, *"Goodnight, Ryan, I love you."* And my brother appropriately responded to her. Then I hear, *"Goodnight, Kerry, I love you."* And, of course, I responded appropriately with, *"I love you, too!"* I continued excitedly to say, *"I love myself!"* I exclaimed. Then I heard the giggles from Ryan and my mother. I, too, giggled and remembered thinking, that was weird to say, but at that moment in my life, I did love myself deeply.

When I think back on this moment, a little embarrassment starts to surface when retelling this story. I mean, who emphatically claims love for themselves? I remember thinking that maybe I was a little strange or weird and that it is not typical to love yourself. In looking back, I feel this was the starting point to the long trek of learning to "unlove" myself. Claiming to love yourself does seem weird and silly to many. To the same many, they are uncomfortable with the idea of you loving yourself, and to the same many people, *they* are uncomfortable with actually loving themselves.

And so it begins. The baton to this relay race of life is exchanged from our culture and society or our family structures, "Here, this will help you." From the moment we are born, we have an innate sense of our worth, our love, and then subtly, over time, or in a grand moment, this tool of measurement, this baton, is handed off to us. I'm not sure where the starting line is for this race through the life of judgment and comparison, and I'm sure it is different for each person. We each have a turn at being measured of our worthiness, and right at that moment, we discount ourselves altogether. We are measuring ourselves against unrealistic expectations in various forms.

Whether it is shiny and glittery or a solid, matte finish, we all have this tool to show our worth. And so, we become accustomed to running through our lives measuring our worth and the relationship of love for ourselves. In this Season of my life, I think back to the sweet, innocent, nine-year-old little girl and how far she has run through this race—enduring all the judgments, expectations, and comparison issues that ruled over her. I tuck her in each night before bed and say, *Kerry Hope, I love you.* And in return, I hear a soft, little whisper back, "I love myself."

Heart Chakra: Lessons on the Journey

My Mother whispers to Me: *"I can see it on your face and in your eyes."*

Me: *"Umm, what?"*

My Mother: *"You're in love!"*

Me: *"Yeah, I mean, I feel like this is pretty obvious to everyone."*

My Mother: *"Mmmm, maybe those in your close circle of women, or rather those you are allowing to be close to you. You have limited a lot of connection with people."*

Me: *"Yeah, I don't know who to trust, or who will even still like me, or hate me, or if I will ever be accepted by family and all of the 'once husband's family.' I guess I am just a bit scared of interacting with the people in my life."*

My Mother: *"Well, there are probably people that are pretty upset with you right now, and let me once again remind you for the one hundredth time, that is THEIR issue, not yours. And that you DO have people who love you more than ever for being honest and truthful. You have to keep loving yourself and keep your heart open to receiving love from others. If you block your Heart Chakra while you are in this mindset that everybody is on the 'other team,' then you will indeed block all the beautiful people, family, and friends in your life from being able to love YOU."*

Me: *"I hear you, I'm trying to keep my heart open, but I am so scared. I am scared of rejection and ridicule and more shaming, more guilt. I just can't handle it. So it is way easier to close off and just be hidden."*

My Mother: *"Yes, love, I know. I understand why you have those feelings. It make sense as to why you are having those feelings. But, trust me when I say to you, you will receive love and support from others. I know this to be true because you give so much love to your children, your girlfriends, and yourself. Love is a continuous wave of motion. You must give to receive. You must receive to give."*

Me: *"This is a beautiful reminder for sure. When I pour in my love to my kids, I can feel the love back in unexpected ways. I AM working so hard to keep my heart open for myself too. But, trust me, the layers of shame are not always easy to diminish, and I keep saying my mantras for forgiveness."*

My Mother: *"My love. Keep doing the work. Keep your heart open. Keep giving love to others, the kids, yourself, and you will see the people who are meant to continue to be in your life showing up for you. Keep in mind, that EVERYONE is also going through some heaviness this Spring. We are all challenged by new ways of living through this pandemic. But, I must say, you found a pretty damn good time to undo your previous life, lady. You and the rest of the world at the same time!"*

Me: *"Yep. It was all perfect, Divine timing, wasn't it."*

My Mother: *"I see how much you are in love. Just keep loving. It will all be okay, I promise."*

LEARNING TO LOVE WITHOUT CONDITIONS

How can we determine if the love we give to others is unconditional? For years, I was in the mindset that I was loved and capable of providing unconditional love. However, once I started to find more contemplation around the topic, I found more depth in the ideals of unconditional love. There are people in your life who you may love but unknowingly have conditions around your love for them. In addition, the people you think genuinely love you unconditionally, well, they just don't. Learning lessons around unconditional love has been incredibly impactful and my most significant life lesson thus far.

We make decisions throughout our lives to give our love to others, whether it be our best friends from middle school, girlfriends/boyfriends in high school, or even perhaps life-long partners. Of course, we can also have various levels of love for each relationship, which I believe we all know. However, it has struck me in traumatic ways how love in certain relationships does have conditions.

I think about how much love my heart can hold for my children, family, girlfriends, dog, and past and current partner. However odd, I found it hard to say that I loved my once husband unconditionally. I wanted to. It felt like I should have been able to do that, but then I thought about the little things that I didn't love. I did have conditions around my love for him. He embraced habits and behaviors that I just did not love. I think about some things he may not have loved about me, behaviors, and patterns I held. I know there were conditions on his love for me as well. You might be thinking, sure, everyone has their minor annoyances in relationships, and that's part of being human, to which I say, you are right!

Being fully in love can be unconditional for some, and I would say it's a challenging feat to accomplish for many. I don't want us to sit in the space of judgment around our love, be it unconditional or not. However, this became an incredibly painful experience; the pain and trauma of discovering that a mother's love isn't unconditional was heartbreaking and raw. Then, I became more aware of how many people go through life without feeling the gift of unconditional love.

As my life changed over many months, I was able to experience unconditional love from some of my closest girlfriends. I share my experience of this as a way for us to be honest about our expectations around love. I also discovered that if we can build a Self-Love practice, we will be able to build unconditional love for ourselves. Self-Love and Self-Care can be at the forefront of our day-to-day. We can build a steadier relationship with ourselves, which will create better foundations in all of our relationships. And when we face moments in our relationships where conditions are apparent, we have a strong sense of love for ourselves, allowing us to endure and continue to love. How magical it would be if we all truly felt unconditional love!

Amid these life changes, one of my best girlfriends from college was very concerned and perhaps very upset over my decision to dismantle an eighteen-year marriage. I would hear her say, *"Kerry, my love for you has no conditions,"* in many hard conversations with her. *"I just want to understand the WHYs."* There was no way around her questions and this complicated conversation; we had to move through it.

At first, I felt that her questions were conditions for our friendship.

From my friend's vantage point, she only witnessed me jump to point D(divorce). She didn't have the context or understanding for how and why I moved from point A to B, to point C, and then finally to D. Rather than just being upset and writing me off from her list of friendships, she continuously made an effort to learn about my "whys." She refused to set any conditions on her love for me. Because my friend took the time to ask the hard questions, eventually, she learned that my drastic life decisions were for the betterment of myself and my happiness.

She clearly meant it when she said, *"I love you without conditions,"* yet still, there were upsetting and confusing questions. I found myself not only grateful for her persistence to learn and understand, but I hold her in the highest regard for a person that can genuinely embrace unconditional love. This friend proved that it is possible by demonstrating love without conditions.

When I think of the term "a mother's love," I quickly think of being held so tightly and so lovingly that it goes hand-in-hand in meaning with unconditional love. When I held each of my newborn babies for the first time, the sensation of limitless love came rushing in for me. Having these little creations of life was one of the greatest honors and moments I have ever experienced. As a mother, you grow alongside these little beings. You learn so much about yourself as they do through all their little chapters of being a toddler, a young child, and early childhood development and adolescence.

As a mother to my two resilient and heartopened children, my main goals and desires are that they will ALWAYS know and feel my unconditional love. May they wake up every morning of their lives, even if they are angry or upset with me, and know that I truly love them unconditionally. I will love them regardless of their choices, and although I am sure they will do their best in all their decision-making, I also am entirely realistic that they will make mistakes from time to time.

Life is for learning, and some of our greatest lessons come in those most challenging moments. I know they will have heartbreaks, heartaches, setbacks, and disappointments. However, I have witnessed these children navigate some super heartbreaking changes in their lives, and through it all, they know they are loved. As I traverse these waters from pre-teen, to teenage, to young adulthood, and beyond, I can already hear myself saying, "My love for you has no conditions; just help me understand."

In some cases, love from a mother does come with conditions. It does come in ways that don't always feel super loving. For me, I found my mother's love always to have a little bit of an edge to it. We used the term "tough love" in the 1980s and 1990s. It was a style of parenting that was encouraged to discipline your children and keep them safe. Growing up in tough-love environments caused harm as a youth and teenager. In truth, not feeling loved by your parents at any stage of life is traumatizing. Over time I have witnessed people who have beautiful, loving relationships with their parents and have learned of those who have never felt any connection or love from a parent their whole life.

In a recent conversation with my friends, we discussed ways to meet our children wherever they are in their lives or circumstances. Let's have a conversation with them to help each other understand better what each of us is feeling. Parenting today shouldn't include shame and guilt or tough-love tactics. How can we advance as parents with compassion? I would have loved to have a mother willing to hear my side of things before issuing a severe repercussion, guilting me, and shaming me for my choices and decisions. Understanding the 'why' is such a radical act of compassion. It can bridge-build healthy relationships with those you love and avoid unnecessary harm and trauma for that person.

Loving without conditions is a human superpower. Can you think of how you can continue to love your partner, friends, or children without setting any boundaries around them to meet your expectations of love? Can we allow each person to live their own human experience without judgment? I often wonder how free we would feel if we didn't spend so much energy and time worrying about our loved ones. Instead, trust that they will continue to be good people by watching you be a good person and feeling your unconditional love.

Let's take it a step further. What would you feel like if you unconditionally loved yourself?

Maybe pause to feel into this question. What conditions do you put on yourself to love yourself?

I know that my list can be hefty and ongoing, and I work so hard not to judge myself. When I'm not productive enough - the "Why" is because I was sleepless all night, and I'm not at total capacity. When I feel unhealthy and have put on extra weight, the "Why" may be that I have been giving all my spare time to work and kid's activities and not making time to work out or go for a walk. Why am I so emotional right now - the "why" is because I am days away from starting a menstruation cycle, and I need to be more gentle with myself. I can always find a "Why" when I am hard on Myself. What if we recognize when we put conditions on our Self-Love? What if we say to ourselves, *"I love you no matter, just help me understand the WHY."*

We can overcome our limitations. We can overcome our conditions of loving ourselves, and it does and will take time and practice. But won't it be so worth it? Imagine how you would feel if you could demonstrate truly loving your Self unconditionally. Think of the impact you would make on those closest to you if you gave them full permission to love themselves. Becoming aware of your love for yourself and being able to show up fully to love another.

The ultimate goal in this life could just be that simple. To love yourself without judgment and to love others the same, without conditions.

Letter to My Maiden, June 2020

Dear Maiden,

How are you, my darling sweetheart? I hope this letter finds you doing great things and living out some epic adventures. I can envision you enjoying the heat of the Summer, laughing with your camp co-workers, and enjoying your life to the fullest.

I've always admired your sense of adventure and your desire to soak in all that life offers. Leading kids on backpacking adventures, white-water rafting, and facilitating rock climbing or ropes course adrenaline rushes. Your leadership and mentoring of the youth through nature and adventurous activities are gifts and talents.

I hope that you always stay true to yourself. No matter who you meet along your path in life, you remember who you are and what you truly stand for. Speak up for those that need advocating. Speak up for yourself when you need support, love, protection, and fun. Whatever you need or desire, please find the courage to take care of your needs.

In turn, I will be sure to always carry your passions and your enthusiasm for life with me for my requests. Your sense of adventure will continue to show up in my life, as I know how important that is to a sun sign Sagittarius Maiden. I promise together, we will never settle for what does not suit us in this short little life we have to live.

Every time I hear the perfect rendition of The Grateful Dead's *"Estimated Prophet"*, I smile and think of you, especially when Donna kicks in "California" at the top of her lungs. It reminds me of our good ol' days of being carefree and living in the Golden State. Thank you for always following the trail of crumbs that have led us on the most epic adventure of life together.

Stay true to you, my dear Maiden. I love you, and I am here for you always. Oh, and you'll never believe how our life shakes out in your forties. It for sure will bring a smile to your face; after all, "there's nothing left to do but smile, smile, smile." *"He's Gone,"* The Grateful Dead

Love to you always,

Kerry Hope

FINDING LOVE OF SELF

Self-Love happens to be one of the most prominent buzzwords across many of my social media channels. More and more authors, poets, artists, yoga gurus and personal or life coaches, and even many therapists I follow speak about Self-Love and how to incorporate more Self-Love practices.

Merriam Webster defines Self-Love simply as "an appreciation of one's own worth or virtue."

Further, Sara M. Bosworth writes, "Self-Love begins when we observe our actions and words with compassion as if we were our own best friend."

However, there also seems to be some trip-ups around the concept of Self-Love versus Selfishness. In my life, some people have misunderstood the sense of care and love that I have for myself and my ability to express it, to be selfish. For me, Self-Care and Self-Love are the farthest things from selfishness. Taking time to prioritize health by working out and finding time to hit a yoga studio class or boxing class is Self-Care and Self-Love. It's the ability to make time for myself. Just me. One of my favorite things to do for myself is sit in a hot sauna. However, I always was made to feel that the time alone was then time away from those that I love. Being in solitude is one of the greatest gifts I give myself. For many, being alone sounds excruciating. I sit in a place of non-judgment around those that cannot do solo time; however, I shouldn't feel that I have to defend my choice of needing solitude.

Now don't get me wrong, I don't know how I could have survived the changes in my life as I did without the love and support from all the amazing women in my life. The connection and exchange of love were invaluable to me. Yet, one person who was with me at every step and moment through this process was Me. How grateful I am to Her! How often did she provide all the love, healing, and support for me? Every single day. So to learn to love yourself and be your own best friend, supporter, and advocate is one of the most incredible Self-Love acts you can make in this life.

When I was about nineteen years old, I bought myself a silver ring for my left hand that I wore continuously for years. It was three rings, all interconnected to make one ring. I remember I would remove it and play around with it as a fidget-widget, especially when I was nervous or taking tests in school. As my rebellious Maiden self, I declared that no matter the boyfriend's situation, I would always wear this ring to remind myself to honor and love my body, my mind and my spiritual connection. I knew the importance of how the interconnection of these rings was so significant to each of those components of Self— Body, Mind, and Spirit. You can't have just one. They all come in a combo pack for the human being. Ahh, very clever Maiden Kerry!

In 2002, my brother, mother, and I took a trip to New York City. A quick weekend get-a-way to enjoy the city and celebrate my mother for Mother's Day. There was a chill in the air, and at this time of the year, you wanted to feel the sun's warmth. We found ourselves after dinner walking a bridge over the Hudson River. Something inside me said *it's time that I release this ring of commitment to myself.* And perhaps it was a sensation of letting go of my old self, my younger rebellious Maiden self. A few months prior, I said "yes" to marriage to a great man. The guy that was going to take care of me and love me for my Body, Mind, and Spirit. I no longer felt I needed that ring as a pact to myself. And so I chucked it! Before I could even wonder if this was the best decision, I saw the three rings representing the love for thyself just fly through the night of the city sky and plop into the river water.

I love the symbolism of this ring, and at this time in my life, I wish that I had realized the metaphor that this ring or series of rings was also infinite. Committing myself to marriage didn't mean that I needed to forgo the love and commitment to myself. Since I have recommitted back to my Self, I have found that I deeply care about all components of my life. Being dedicated to healthier ways of living through my Body, Mind, and Spirit was the best *I do* I have ever spoken.

When we can release judgments of ourselves, or at least start to become aware of our judgments of Self, then we can make room in ourselves for more love. Our judgments can block others from seeing our best versions of ourselves. These recommitments can also take time, and building a Self-Care and Self-Love practice is the only place to start. Self-Love is invaluable to our everyday lives and can be a reminder of eternal love to our ourSelves.

The ring symbolizes endings and beginnings and how cyclical our love can be for ourselves. We can fall in and out of love with ourselves. We can drop in and out of love with others, too. In both cases, you can always come back to love yourself. You can show your heart how possible it is to fall back in love with others. The possibilities of loving yourself will unfold in so many other beautiful ways to experience love in this world.

I AM LOVE:
A SWEET CONVERSATION WITH SELF

I love you.

I speak this in a whisper so that my ears can hear the words.

I mean it, I love you.

I am feeling deeper into my own source of love for me.

I am here to listen.

I reassure myself so that I know what exactly it is that I need.

How can I help you?

I learn how to nurture the very being within my Soul that yearns for love.

There, there, my dear.

I touch my cheeks with a gentle touch.

I am love.

I place my hands on my chest to feel my beating heart and the breath in my chest.

You are loved.

I feel my belly and the insecurities inside, and I acknowledge the sensation.

We are love.

You are made of a million particles of love in your body. You have a heart full of love, a mind that creates beautiful thoughts, and a belly full of wisdom.

I am love.

You are loved.

We are love.

And remember, when it feels as if every person has turned their back on you, I am still here. I will always be here. Oh, and by the way, the dog still loves you, too.

CONNECTING TO YOUR MAIDEN WISDOM: VISUALIZATION

Before you read this next section, please find yourself in a place of peace and solitude. Have a journal and pen nearby (or use this book to jot down any notes) so that you may capture any wisdom you gain as you connect to your inner knowing from your Mother and Crone archetypes.

Pause now to close your eyes, and take three slow, deep, long, rich breaths in and out.

As you settle into yourself, begin by noticing all your sensations around your body. What does your clothing feel like on your skin? Are you warm, or is there a chill in the air? What smells do you notice around you? How does this book feel in your hands or on your lap? Step yourself through all five senses of your being.

How, at this moment, are you caring for your personal needs? Adjust yourself accordingly, and provide any additional comforts for yourself. For example, are your toes covered with cozy socks or a blanket? Do your shoulders feel wrapped up and secure? Or do you need a gentle breeze of a fan to keep you cool?

Regardless of the Season of Life you are in at this moment, your inner Maiden helped to create the foundation for who you are in this life. Your inner Maiden is always here to remind you of how far you have come and honor how much she endured.

As you reflect on a memory of being in your Maiden years of life, you suddenly hear loud music playing, which catches your attention and brings a smile to your face. The lyrics of this song remind you of when you were a young teenager, and this song was your anthem. The song or artist was your absolute favorite, and you played this album, tape, or CD over and over again.

What song or artist do you hear?

You get up and begin to move your body, and you notice that you are dancing and moving the way your younger version of Self would dance. You find yourself laughing and feeling ridiculous but remembering what it was like to be carefree. You follow the music's sound to a door covered with posters and photos - what images do you see as you gently tap on the door?

The door flings open, and the music is now really loud, and you are greeted by your Maiden. She smiles and offers for you to come into her room. You are instantly reminded of what your bedroom was like when you were a teenager. What do you recall? Are there posters on the walls? What was your bed frame or the color of your bedding? Was there a significant stuffed animal that you still adored from your early childhood sitting on a shelf? Was there a phone on which you talked to your girlfriends or boyfriends? Is the room messy with clothes or tidy? What other details stand out to you as you find your way to the edge of the bed to sit with your Maiden self?

She lowers the volume of your favorite song and speaks, "I'm glad you are here. I have been waiting for your attention. I just wanted to say that I am so proud of you for getting to this point in your life. You have done a really great job."

How does this feel to hear? Are you feeling a sense of relief? Do you nod your head in agreement? What other feelings come to your heart?

This sparks a response in your heart, and what then do you say back to Her?

Use this moment to share with your Maiden self all you wish you would have heard in this stage of life. What advice could you share? What wisdom would have helped her?

Congratulate her on her successes. Or give her grace and forgiveness for her mistakes.

As you finish up all your loving thoughts and words to share with this young version of yourself, you lean in to give her a warm embrace. You can feel her body melt into your arms with so much love and admiration. What other sensations are you noticing in your body?

After a nice, long hug, you both simultaneously stand up and giggle slightly as you see each other teary-eyed. You grab her hands, and you have one last piece of advice or words of encouragement that you feel called to speak to her now. What do you want her to know?

You turn toward the bedroom door and begin to leave when your Maiden speaks,

"Wait! I just want you to always remember . . ."

What is it that you have forgotten that she reminds you of at this time?

Your heart is full of this remembrance, and you smile in gratitude toward her and slowly shut the bedroom door. As you walk back to your space, you can hear the music start to play again, and your body starts to move and dance as if nobody is watching.

Take the time now to write down any message that your Maiden shared with you. What did she want you to remember? Or, take a moment to write a letter to your Maiden self. What would you say to her now?

You can always connect to your Maiden in any season of the year or any Season of Life.

She is always with you.

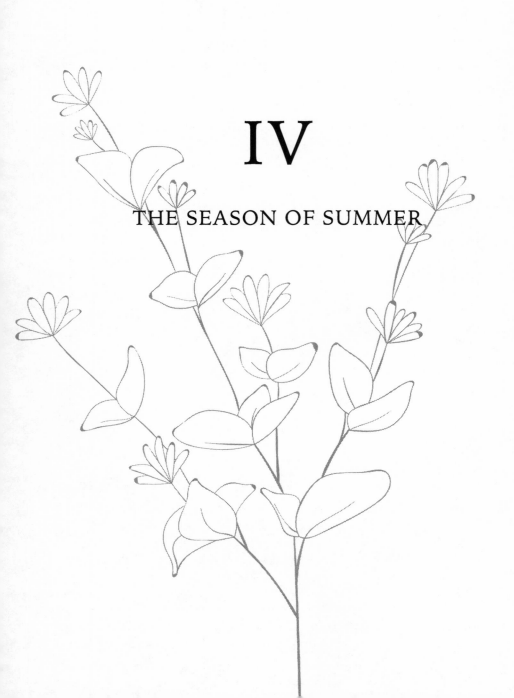

IV

THE SEASON OF SUMMER

HONORING YOUR SOUL'S PATH & YOUR TRUTH

We are now feeling into the fullness of this Summer Season, allowing the heat to burn within our Soul Beings. We thrive when we can feel into our passions and recognize the unique fuel formulas that inspire us as individuals. Shine on, Sister. Now is the time to shine like the sun.

The fullness and abundance around this planet in the Summer Season is a beautiful reminder of how we are all full of beautiful bounty. Our planet Earth, which many refer to as Mother, demonstrates that the Mother archetype can indeed hold so much. The Mother is abundant in the amount of love she can give. Similarly, our planet Earth continues to provide and give.

So we can find moments this Season to feel into the bounty of love we have for each other, the love we have for our planet, and the love that we can give to ourselves.

Allow your arms to fly freely into the air, walk barefoot in lush grasses, feel the coolness of the waters, and fully expose yourself to the greatness of the Mother that resides within you!

Letter to Mother, July 2020

Dear Mother,

The essence of your immense love is so incredible as I feel it surrounding me at this time. The heat of Summer has created such warmth in my Soul, and the feeling of your energetic embrace heals my heart. Thank you for your love and support, which carries me through to the other side of this transition.

The moments of joy feel surreal now that I am back in my lover's arms again. Being back in communication with her daily brings me hope.

However, I am still experiencing moments of pain, grief, and shame as I continue to move through this Season of Separation, but I have sensations of freedom all around me this time. I am grateful for my space in this new home and for my heart.

Throughout my day, I feel unstable, and I use your strength to breathe through the moments when I get taken down or hijacked emotionally. I feel lucky to have the tools to get back on my feet each time.

Thank you for being the sounding board for all my pains and stories. I know as a mother, it is excruciating to witness your children go through painful experiences. Thank you for being a witness and allowing me to feel the security of your devotion.

The love from a Mother is one of the greatest loves to receive. Yet this Season, I have found more joy and healing for myself in the very act of giving. Thank you for showing me how to love so big and give that same love to my own two children as they are going through their own painful time from the separation.

I am making my new house feel like a home. We are creating new memories just the three of us, and although I wonder if they can see the pain on my face, I know they, too, are adjusting to a whole new life and way of living. The feeling of being responsible can be overbearing at times. So I find sweet moments in the afternoon to rest on my bed, then get up and make a delicious dinner. I am taking two steps forward, knowing that I might stumble back

with every step. Thank you, Mother, for showing me
how to keep walking through the pain.

Lots of love to you,

Kerry Hope

Heart Chakra: Lessons on the Journey

My Mother whispers to Me: *"Good morning, my friend! It's a beautiful Summer day. The birds are chirping, the grass is sparkling with morning dew, and you are still laying in bed with a pillow over your head. What's up?"*

Me: *"Uuugh. I just can't today."*

My Mother: *"Oh, stop it. Stop feeling bad for yourself, and get your butt out of bed. You were the one who wanted a new life for yourself, AND you had to get out from under all that control."*

Me: *"It would have been easier to stay."*

My Mother: *"Yes, and for many women, they do stay, and men stay too. Unhealthy and toxic relationships are unbearable to the heart in many ways, and what you are learning is that it is hard and feels unbearable. And you know what, my friend, it will get easier."*

Me: *"I keep hearing those words from all my friends, but why then am I always taken down and still allow the manipulation to affect me?"*

My Mother: *"Well, how are you doing at protecting your Heart Chakra energy? When you are open and allow healthy ways to protect yourself, you can better determine what will and what will not affect you."*

Me: *"I'm trying so hard to stay open and gentle with myself. My heart is still healing, and I'm trying to protect it, but he is so pissed and angry and finds ways to make me feel weak and continues to talk to me like I am an idiot for not going back to fix the marriage. It's exhausting, and I honestly think it would be easier to go back than to deal with the constant overpowering tactics."*

My Mother: *"Stop allowing it, Kerry! You know you have the tools to stop him in his tracks. Stop the conversations, and ground yourself down. Let's review the Heart Visualization you learned in Wild & Awake training, shall we? Come on, Sit up.*

Now, focus on your Root Chakra first. Breathe there.

See your body tethered into the core of the earth.

Then move up to your Sacral, breathe in the essence of your sense of Self, what are you creating in this world for yourself, see yourself thriving, dancing, making love, and being free.

Pause there.

Now, power up through your Solar Plexus.

Breath here for a moment and feel all of the strength you carry.

Visualize yourself in your full power, warrior mode. Breath into what it would feel like to stay 'NO' loudly and mean it.

No more power over you.

No more manipulation.

No more gas-lighting.

No more shaming.

No more guilting you.

You are NOT taking it anymore.

Now, take three slow, deep breaths.

Visualize yourself as strong as a large oak tree. Solid, grounded, and secure.

You can protect your heart when all your lower chakras are open.

Now, visualize a single rose in front of your body, your tree.

This beautiful, sacral orange rose is the protector of your heart.

This rose is what will absorb all the negative energy people are throwing your way. YOU, Kerry Hope, are the protector of your own heart and well-being. You choose to better life for yourself and, ultimately, your kids.

Keep breathing. And when you feel complete, you can open your eyes.

You've got this, Kerry Hope. Keep going."

NURTURING AND ALLOWING LOVE

When we can connect to our hearts, to our essence, and feel the sensation of love for our Self, it is in this place that we allow ourselves to be loved by others. When we can love and value our worth, it is then that we can find healthy ways to be in love with and be nurtured by others.

This Season of Summer brings deep love and nurturing. I was falling madly in love with this beautiful woman, who held my hand when I asked and released it when I needed the space. She was my rock of strength and often had to pick me up in my down moments of sadness. Additionally, she witnessed me grow with the sun's light into a beautiful new Being.

I had never been intimate or loved by a woman before; this was a whole new experience. Being loved and nurtured by a woman is truly an incredible experience for me. The softness in her words and touch, the care that comes from behind her eyes. The way she would just hold me in moments of joy and sorrow. She and I have a connection that words cannot describe. There is an intuitive knowing we have for each other, which allows for us to be fully open and vulnerable in all ways.

Her love for me was a healing balm to my Soul. Her love gave me the courage to keep going each day and the hope for a beautiful future together. Although we lived in different cities, and our schedules only allowed us to be in person every few weeks, we continued to fall in love more and more each day. In review, I know that I had to show up for myself, forgive, and continue to love myself as I was changing. For me to feel her love, to allow her to nurture me, I had to be able to do the same for myself. I had to let myself feel and see how I could give back love to her in a way I never knew was possible.

I believe that people exchange love with each other in many different ways. Just as you can fall in and out of love with another person, you can fall in and out of love with yourself as well. I can recall moments and times when I was not connected to my own heart. I know that it has been a winding road for me to see myself in the light of love. However, when I allow Soul and Heart connection, I also am able to receive the love from others, my partner, my parents, my children, my friends, and myself.

We hold the key to our receiving. We are the ones that can allow the love to flow, and it has to start with knowing your own heart and loving your Self.

RECEIVING LOVE FROM MY SOUL FAMILY

It was in my knowing that I was still worthy of being loved through this life transition. I nurtured my heart connection. I knew that I had to be open to love and nurturing love differently. I had to create a new family to care for me. I felt as if I had lost so many people who were important to me as I reimagined and reconstructed my life. The abandonment that I felt from friends and my family was debilitating at times. Still, I continued to fight and keep my connection to my heart strong.

I also knew that I had to reach outward and foster love with my new Soul family. I knew that my container of Sisters, which included my closest girlfriends, was at my nuclear core, so I started there. I felt their love, I felt their support, and slowly over time and gatherings, their partners and husbands offered their love and support, too.

This love and acceptance from other men were potent for me to feel. In my mind, I had been projecting my thoughts onto other people. So for me to know that my friend's husband didn't see me as a *crazy woman who left her husband for another woman* reassured my sense of security. Instead, they were men who truly supported women to be authentic, open, and honest. There was no "Bro-code" they were breaking by supporting me and my journey. They saw me for me, and they continued to love me. Men that were secure in their sense of Self were also able to give love to my new partner. These were the men of my Soul Family. I hold them sacred.

In addition, my friend's children have adjusted their lens, seeing me as the same mother to two great kids, and are now happy with a new partner who is a woman. I learned quickly that my friends had raised their children to be open-hearted and open-minded. Overall, it's safe to say that I feel our society's vast changing landscape of acceptance is also a factor.

Several of my closest friends shared their conversations with their kids who have felt emotions and curiosity about bi-sexuality, pan-sexuality, and homosexuality. Teenagers of my Soul family are transitioning through to the opposite of their birth genders, and as parents, we are all learning new pronouns and referring to their once daughter as he/him. Through this transition, my two children, resilient and happy, have also found new ways to love and be loved by more than just their mother and father. I am forever grateful for my two fabulous, accepting, and forgiving kids—what a gift for our entire Soul family and me.

My chosen Soul family is loving, accepting, non-judgemental, safe, and secure; their hearts are open and have welcoming homes. These same values are the essence my partner and I have created for our home. We are, in a sense, in control of how we create, gather, and nurture the relationships within our Soul family. I have learned that I can choose to honor certain people and relationships as a means of "family." And this has been one of my greatest lessons.

Throat Chakra: Lessons on the Journey, Ignoring Your Inner Knowing

Me: *The lessons around a blocked Throat Chakra came to me from all three of my archetypes throughout the years. Maiden, Mother, and Crone were all present in each of the ways I chose not to speak up. I heard their voices in my heart even when I didn't act on them. At these moments in my life, I was not brave enough to speak up, to share how I was truly feeling. It was easier to just go along with it.*

Me: When I allow jokes to be made about me in front of friends and family, knowing just about everything is up for grabs as a topic of dinner conversation. So, again, just laugh it off so that no one feels awkward or gets upset. Yep, I got it. *"Just keep laughing, Kerry, if they are laughing and you are laughing, then none of this will feel weird, awkward, or unkind."*

My Crone Speaks Up: *"That is not okay for you to say or poke fun at my way of being and important things to me. I will no longer tolerate you making fun of me in front of my friends at gatherings. It is hurtful, embarrassing, and frankly disrespectful."*

Me: Let him order your meal. After years of being criticized for "ordering the wrong thing" because his choice was the better option, I decided to let him order all the food for me. Therefore during many meals, I sat disappointed in front of undercooked raw, red meat.

My Mother Speaks Up: *"Hey, thanks for the suggestion on the prime rib, but that is not a food I enjoy eating. I think the Ahi Tuna salad is my choice for the meal."*

Me: Regardless of how certain behaviors don't align with my values and my true nature, just keep quiet. I have witnessed other women feel awkward or violated by others, and not speaking up in those moments leaves me feeling responsible. A behavior is gone in the next moment, and this too will pass.

My Maiden: *"No, these violations of my values and true nature are a hard boundary, NO! I will not contort myself so vigorously in order to be in relationship or accepted by others."*

Me: I wonder how different my life would be if I had been able to set more boundaries for myself. Would my marriage have lasted as long as it did? Or possibly not have fallen out of love with a partner that did not validate my choices? Would I hold resentment in my heart if I had just been clear on my communication?

We are all living in the context of our environment. Behaviors are both learned and chosen. I can use my voice to extricate myself from situations where I do not feel valued or loved. I have the sovereignty within me to make new choices and to speak my truth.

SETTING AND HOLDING BOUNDARIES

Creating the life your Soul needs comes with one of the most difficult – and for me, the most challenging – components of living a healthy life: setting boundaries. I speak on this topic as a student, not a master. Yet, I continue to learn and demonstrate healthy boundaries every day of my life. Some days I can high-five myself for my ability to communicate and set boundaries. On other days I feel less than successful. When I struggle, I remember that I have many days in front of me. I can continue communicating, finding better ways to express my boundaries and why they are essential.

There are so many great boundary-setting resources through books, podcasts, articles and blogs, and even quick tips on social media. There is unlimited support if you want to learn the best approach to setting boundaries. However, it can be very challenging to create a boundary for yourself.

I always thought that I was a person that could say what I liked, didn't like, needed, didn't need, etc. I believe that I am very vocal about how to meet all my needs. However, over time I allowed certain people to walk and talk all over me. Often I found I would "comply" with the majority to keep the peace or appear easygoing. This seems like a kinder approach, but I have learned that by allowing others to dominate these situations, I have been very unkind to myself. And that is how I came to understand the phrase, that clear *communication is KIND*.

When you communicate your feelings and thoughts, you help those around you to understand your point of view and the reason behind your behavior. The saying goes, *You only know what you only know*. So it's hard to be upset with a partner, spouse, or family member if you don't speak your needs and thoughts.

Communication is the cornerstone for setting boundaries—communication with Self and others. I am learning that setting boundaries are so freaking hard because people tend not to like it when you set limits and expectations that accommodate your needs. This is especially difficult when you start setting boundaries in long-standing relationships where you have not practiced establishing limitations for many years.

When a person you have formulated a relationship with then changes the dynamics of that relationship, it can be confusing and frustrating. I began to improve my life experiences by speaking up about my feelings about situations. The people who were not accustomed to me speaking up became uncomfortable when they could not control the outcome. Setting boundaries is complex, complicated, and challenging for both participants. It takes time to get into a rhythm when changing patterns and behaviors in all ways. I am still learning how to set new boundaries and then reset them repeatedly if necessary.

In relearning how to use my voice on topics that are important to me, I have realized the amount of dialogue available around setting boundaries. Many people, like me, struggle with supporting their own needs, voice, and opinions in their close relationships. I wish there were a magical solution to overcoming boundary setting. The only thing I can do is keep practicing and reassuring myself. To be in healthy relationships with all my friends, family, co-workers, and partner, I need to be clear. Clear communication is Kind.

While I was learning the art of boundary setting, almost everyone in the United States also learned how to deal with boundaries being set on us collectively. Through the COVID-19 pandemic, many people felt the discomfort of limitations placed on our daily lives and routines. In addition, we all had to learn the skill of setting boundaries to keep us healthy and safe. It became almost a universal practice. We had barriers in our work environments, how we shopped for groceries, and how we socialized with family and friends. Unknowingly, many of us had limitations placed on us during this time. It was a lesson for us all to feel what it was like to have boundaries set on us individually and collectively.

Setting boundaries is not an easy practice, but it is a simple one we all must learn to thrive in healthy ways. Setting boundaries for yourself can be as simple as opting out of a large group gathering. On the other hand, it can be as complex as saying, *"I don't deserve to be shamed or spoken to with unkind words and harsh tones; therefore, I am ending this relationship."*

The spectrum of setting boundaries is vast, and finding ways to practice this skill is an endless endeavor. We have all experienced limits placed on us with our global pandemic. It is also imperative that we keep an open heart to those in our lives who create new boundaries for themselves. Be willing to understand where they are coming from, and perhaps a little more understanding of the courage it takes.

THE ART OF BEING FLUID

In my daily practice of using oracle message cards, I have become fond of a particular deck of cards, The Spirit Animal Oracle (Colette Baron-Reid). Each card beautifully illustrates an animal and the spiritual message they are teaching. For example, when I pulled the card of the dolphin, the message was, "This and that is true." The dolphin swims through dark waters and comes up to the surface light. It enjoys both *this and that:* the duality of life. Not everything is black or white. In all our beautifully messy ways of living, the world is also this and that, and not everything is set in stone in one specific way.

The idea that the dolphin can swim through both *this and that* can also mean that we can change and alter our lifestyles as we flow. Sometimes our limitations might be:

"I cannot give my time to volunteer with the PTA this year and will have to say no when asked to help with the fundraising." It can then switch to: "Now that my kids are through school, I have more free time and would like to dedicate more time volunteering to an organization that fuels my passion." We can establish patterns for ourselves, and then we can change them. Certain days of the week are dedicated to working out, and the other days are for relaxation.

The art of being fluid is just that, a skill that only YOU can design and create for yourself.

There were chapters of my life when I was a vegetarian. I mostly ate grilled cheese, avocado subs, and french fries during these times: basically unhealthy college-style eating without meat. Then there were years of eating meat. Then, I decided not to eat meat after leaving my marriage and found a lifestyle of vegetarianism but in a healthier way this time. After this lifestyle change, I realized there was a way to incorporate well-sourced animal protein into my diet that didn't make me sick. Eating this way enables me to feel more energized and thrive better throughout my days. Had I stuck with one lifestyle for myself, I could have become unhealthy and potentially caused harm to myself.

Being mindful of the fluidity in life allows us to monitor our work-life balance, relationships with partners or spouses, and how we spend our social time with friends. There may be moments spent mindlessly scrolling social media, and then you decide to delete the app on your phone for a few weeks to take a break. Even being aware of your fluidity with your intake of news and media.

Feel into your daily routines. Is there something that can be adjusted in your lifestyle that is no longer serving you? Take a moment to feel into the ocean depths of yourself, and ask, how can I be more fluid in my life? Could new lifestyle variations be easily adapted into my daily routine? Allow yourself the comfort and freedom to know that nothing in your life has to be *this or that*. Instead, you can create a middle path in your life that incorporates all aspects you wish to include – even if they may feel contradictory at times.

The gift of fluidity was imperative to my healing process. I could adapt specific tools and practices, meditations, or body movements into my life that helped me in the moment and Season. Yet, not all of the methods carry me through each Season. I found that fluidity allowed me to do what my Soul needed and pivot out of a routine once it felt complete.

The art of fluidity helped me gain confidence that I was listening to my needs and my ability to adapt, which brought growth. Finding ways to implement this practice was empowering to me. It was another way I gained a sense of control and self-worth. I lived in the emotional waters similar to the dolphin. Swimming in and out of light and dark all Summer long.

KNOWING YOUR TRUTH

It seems simple, right? I should know my truth. That seems simple enough. I mean, who else is going to know my truth but me? However, sometimes our "truths" are hidden beneath a veneer of false truth that those around us have manipulated.

For years I thought I was living in complete alignment with myself and the truth of who I am. Well, at least I thought I knew who I was. I was an avid yoga enthusiast. I have had a meditation practice off and on for years. I have strong, independent women friends who were all standing in their power, so I was standing in my power too, right? I was in tune with my spiritual beliefs and practices, and sometimes my alignment with my beliefs made other family members uncomfortable. From my perspective, I have always expressed my thoughts and feelings openly for the most part and often lead my life and career with confidence.

It's hard to know where, when, how, or why I began to hide my truth. I don't think I could pick one moment in time where my "truth" was evident to me, but then I made a conscious choice to go against it. Through this Season of my life, I have learned that I had thoughts and feelings about my sexuality and unmet desires that I was able to negotiate. I could categorize it as if this knowledge was not mine to hold. That's someone else's truth, or maybe it is my truth, but not until later in life, "God forbid anything would happen to my husband or marriage."

My truth could have been something that was deep-seated inside of me but bloomed over time. My truth could have been one of those mind puzzles where you see either a vase or a woman's face depending on how your eyes set on the image. However, the timing and the realization of my truth about my bi-sexuality are what have set me free.

I often looked for my purpose and truth in various modalities, from yoga retreats, self-help books, classes, and spiritual workshops. Seeking my truth has always been something I desired. In all of my discoveries, I have realized that many humans on planet Earth really can't say what their *truth* means. When we adopt a daily practice of speaking up on what we know to be TRUE, we have more insight into our Soul's truthful unfolding. Further, I would say that using our voices to speak up on what we believe to be right or wrong is in governance to our Self and not for other people. We can begin to live in sync with our essence of Self and not follow the herd to the pastures of self-doubt, confusion, or inauthenticity.

In my self-discovery, a big lesson was also learning that my truth is not everyone's truth. Your truth is not the same as mine either. In one of the several couple's counseling sessions, I heard my once husband say, "*Well, what about my truth?*" It was upsetting at the time, as I felt invalidated for my side of the story. As I had to sit with his question, I realized that he, too, is allowed to have a different 'truth' to the story. My growth came when I realized that he would adamantly campaign his truth to all of our family and friends. His truth allowed others to see him as the victim, as he did too. Growth for me was reassuring myself and my heart daily that I could accept my responsibility in our situation that he could not accept. During this Season, I relied heavily on my mantras of self-worth and reassurance to keep me going. My Crone would often whisper, 'the truth is always revealed.'

In our American society, individual truths are as different as we all are from each other. It takes a ton of courage to be able to hear people's truths without judgment. Instead, focus on what's true for you. Accept your own truths and accept that there will be people who have different truths than yours. Release yourself from the constant judgments of others. Stay open to acceptance and non-judgment. If we can all embed this into our Souls, the world will shift miraculously.

DECISION MAKING:
A RADICAL SELF-LOVE ACT

Growing up, my parents provided a safe place and sounding board where I could share my ideas and thoughts. My father always welcomed my creative ideas, as he, too, was a person that loved to dream and scheme. My mother, who was also my boss for twenty years, was a part of many of my decisions. She and my brother provided a lot of counsel for me throughout my life. I wonder if my family perhaps unintentionally enabled my poor decision-making skills by making decisions for me. I could not make any decision by myself without my mother, brother, or once husband's approval or acceptance. I knew I was a bad decision-maker. Picking out clothes to buy or what salads to order, I was in a constant state of struggle around decision-making for what I could feel was the majority of my adult life.

My mother has told me, as a little girl, that I would have tried on four to five different outfits each morning before I could settle on one mismatched shirt and pants. Perhaps I was brought into this world as an indecisive Being as a means to overcome it. Maybe if I had learned to make my own decisions earlier, I would have found a completely different path. As I learned to rely on others when faced with a decision, I also internalized that the people around me didn't think I could make decisions independently. Over time, I began to believe that as well. In doing so, I was telling myself each day that I didn't care or love myself enough to advocate or stand up for what I truly desired.

I have also contemplated whether or not my indecisiveness led me into certain relationships. Was I drawn to people who would make my decisions for me, or were these people drawn to me because they could ultimately sense that I would be easy to control? Allowing others to be in control of my life eventually made me feel loved and also lovable. The essential truth behind my lack of decision-making was that I told myself that I was easygoing and could go with the flow. Letting everyone else decide how things played out was a way for me to stay safe and not upset anyone who had stronger opinions.

The decision to leave my marriage was by far the most radical act of Self-Love and independence I had made in my entire life. This decision affected every aspect of my own life and the lives of others that I love dearly.

When your heart and Soul are shouting for you to take a running leap off a giant mountain with no certainty of where and how you will land, making that choice is terrifying. Making a life-altering decision like this requires that you acknowledge your worthiness while also embracing the courage to make a run for it.

I knew that I was in love with one person, and I had fallen out of love with another. So a decision had to be made to create a new life. The decision to be truthful about my love affair, and my decision to be honest, was pivotal for me to overcome this tendency to be controlled by others. It ultimately came to me making my own decision. And as much pain as that decision had created, it was the only way I could genuinely honor my worth and honor my Self-Love.

If we can see how important the link is between decision-making and self-worthiness, we also can be aware that making our own decisions is indeed a radical act of Self-Love.

Learning to make decisions on my own has been interesting for me. Since I left my marriage and found emancipation for my own Self-governing, I have had to make all kinds of decisions on my own. This has allowed me to tap into my intuition and listen to what I know and what I FEEL to be true. As I review my path, I can see how many of my decisions have been made with confidence and knowing that I am supported when I choose and lead from my heart.

It turns out that decision-making as an act of Self-Love indeed can be strengthened with practice. Start by making small decisions with full awareness and attention. Bring awareness to how you make decisions:

- What is your process when you are faced with a meaningful decision?
- What does it feel like in your body?
- Notice if you become anxious, or can you sense joy when you decide on something that feels "right" to you?

Notice the outcomes of your choices, both the small and big ones. When you start to pay attention to your decision-making experience, you can tap into your power of intuition. We all can use our intuition and wisdom to identify our needs, feelings, cravings, and longings when making decisions.

How can you genuinely honor your intuition and self-worth? When you are in tune with your intuition, you will be amazed at how you make the best choices and decisions for yourself in each moment. So be present to yourself and notice how you feel in this radical act of Self-Love.

Third Eye/Inner Knowing Chakra: Lessons on the Journey

My Mother whispers to Me: "*There you are!*"

Me: "*Oh hello, you startled me.*"

My Mother: "*You look so different. Not only physically has your body changed this Season, but you just feel so different to be around.*"

Me: "*Well, as I sit out here in the heat of the sun and nourish my body with fresh foods, I guess I do feel different. I am finding more moments to be with myself. I always had a hard time finding time to be alone before.*"

My Mother: "*I know, my dear. I used to pray that you would find more time alone to connect back to yourself. You hear yourself better when you honor moments of solitude.*"

Me: "*I have learned over the years that my more profound moments of self-discovery have been in nature and when I've been alone. I love it when I can tap into my sense of Self, inner knowing, and heart.*"

My Mother: "*I can recall these beautiful moments in your life, sweet Kerry. You have created so many peaceful moments by just being present to your surroundings and yourself. Thank you for honoring yourself in such an endearing way.*"

Me: "*Aw, thank you for seeing me.*"

My Mother: "*In these moments of solitude and presence, I hope you are also aware that you are in the most ideal and perfect space to receive the messages your Soul needs to hear.*"

Me: "*Yes, I do know, but often I forget how valuable that is for me at this time of life. I find it easy to fill my time with tasks, chores, work, and kids. I am guilty of not making more time to sit in my meditation practice or be contemplative.*"

My Mother: "*Keep finding the time, my dear. You have to keep the energy channel open in your Third Eye Chakra or inner knowing. You have great wisdom within, and right now, you feel a little alone and abandoned by many people in your life. People are confused about your decisions this past Season, so please take more time to be with yourself. You are no longer running a packed social calendar and schedule. Let me remind you that this is what you were craving, more solitude, peace, and presence. So take advantage of your time this Season. Be alive in every moment you have. Get outside. Be open to all your inner-knowing, and you will find your heart will slowly heal. Your sense of worth will become clear again, and you, my dear, will be okay. I promise."*

WILLINGNESS TO GROW AND LEARN

In this Season of Life, grant me the strength to keep growing.

In this Season of Life, grant me the ability to see all that I endure through the lens of a student.

In this Season of Life, grant me the love for all the awareness I gain for my Self without judgment.

We are all created from the same cellular matter that makes up the plants and trees. How can we expect the life of a tree to grow and change but not expect the same for ourselves? How can we not grow and learn from our life experiences? It just isn't possible unless you prohibit your awareness around the changes of life, around the changes of the Seasons. There has to be a willingness to see the growth and see how you change without allowing others to prohibit or make you feel wrong for growth and evolution.

I recall my mother once told me that she and my father separated and eventually divorced because they continued to grow into different people. I found comfort in that reasoning. When I embarked on marriage to my husband, I was so sure that we would NOT have that reason which to worry. I was convinced that we would grow, change, and develop into beautiful humans together, aligned in our relationship. I never thought that growing and changing would lead me to marriage separation. I believe that some people can grow and change to continue to foster a loving relationship. Conversely, I think that some marriages can remain healthy and strong in their entirety because each person remains in the status quo of each other.

I have always been a seeker and have wanted to grow and develop into more awareness and enlightenment. I cannot be sure that my husband had the same goals. However, the truth is that he continued to grow into a different person, too. He found new hobbies, interests, and friends in which he found his true happiness and belonging. People change. People find growth in places that may not always align with their partner, husband, or wife. For those people that can continue to make a lifestyle and partnership work together in these cases, I very much commend the ability and dedication.

Looking back, I found myself at the crossroads of being able to continue down a path that I knew was not bringing me joy, contentment, and personal growth. I knew that I would be sacrificing my beliefs to fit in and adapt to the mindsets of my husband's new community with which I socialized regularly. Was giving up my marriage to break these constraints for myself worth the heartache and trauma? The answer was and will always be a HELL YES! As I tried to fit in, bought into the beliefs, and tried to dim myself down to fit the mold of an ideal wife, I felt the fire inside of me burn with anger. I looked in a mirror at a woman I couldn't even recognize.

My growth in this life is essential to me. Knowing how I want to be in this world, how I want to feel, how I want to love, how I want to be of service, and how I want to create a legacy has everything to do with making the sacrifice to be true to myself. Being true to my growth and not turning my back on what I know to be true. Does this seem selfish in the eyes of those that were in my circle of family and friends? Perhaps. However, I will never regret demonstrating my dedication to growth and learning to my children. I gave them the gift of sovereignty. I am showing them that they do not have to sacrifice their sense of being, knowing, and trusting their values to fit into a lifestyle.

May I teach my children, and anyone else watching, that being in alignment with your truth, growth, and learning is the ultimate reason we are here on this life journey. May we all understand the lessons that feed ourselves and our Souls. May we not resist the lessons we have come here to learn in this lifetime. One of my best friends always reminds me of the Carl Jung quote, "What you resist not only persists but will grow in size." I don't want to resist my learning or lessons, so they repeatedly keep coming back to me. I want to be the best student possible, learn what I need to know, and move on to a great, more easeful way of living.

As I continue to adopt this way of living, you, too, can find the willingness to learn and grow.

Don't stay complacent.

Keep growing.

Keep going.

Keep rising.

CONNECTION TO SELF AND YOUR COMMUNITY

To honor our most genuine essence of who we are and how we want to show up in this world, as people, women, mothers, Sisters, friends, daughters, co-collaborators, neighbors, partners, and wives, we must take the time to commune with our higher Self. Sitting in meditation, walks in nature, time on the yoga mat, driving alone in your car in silence, a hot tea in a sacred space of your home, or digging around the garden. There are endless ways you can be fully present to yourself. Be fully present to your thoughts, ideas, desires, wishes, needs, creative genius, and even the little whispers of gratitude that your Soul wants you to hear. Make the time to connect to your Self.

We are all in a constant state of transition through our lives and the Seasons, whether we want it or not, whether we like it, and whether we are present. Connecting to Self is a way that creates more ease around these life transitions. When you can be present to yourself in daily practice, there seems to be less resistance to the inevitable shifts and changes.

I look back on all the Seasons of my life, and I can recall all kinds of moments of connecting to myself. In these little moments in my life path, I can pull out the essence of what I need. However, I can also recall memories of my life when I refused to listen to my inner knowing. In turn, I could not fulfill my Soul's needs and rebelled against my heart's desires, my body's needs, or against my better judgment. This reflection exercise can be challenging, embarrassing, humbling, frustrating, and annoying. However, the antidote in these reflections always comes back to love. I was allowing forgiveness and seeing that I was doing the best I could in those moments.

"There, there, sweet Maiden, Kerry. I see you are not showing up in your best way. I see you. I see that you were also doing what you thought was best, and even though the outcome of the situation was not ideal, I now know that you have the skills and experience to know what is best for you."

Suppose we can continue to practice loving-kindness and forgiveness for ourselves. Suppose we stay true to who we want to be in this world and how we show up for ourselves and all the people in our lives. In that case, we will hopefully find fewer ways of disappointing ourselves and each other.

Know who you are, and stay connected to yourself.

This practice requires effort. Find the small moments in your life each day to do this exercise. Find time to listen to your thoughts and heart. The first step? Ask yourself how you best connect with your intuitive wisdom and your body. Experiment with body movements such as walking, running, dancing, swimming, bike riding, or yoga. Alternately, play with stillness and quiet. Journal with a pen and notebook, or use a laptop to release your inner thoughts. Honoring yourself will be one of the greatest gifts you will ever give and will ever receive.

Taking it a step further, how can you support the people in your life to do the same. For example, encouraging your partners to take solo time and kids to have quiet moments without technology to color or create. Supporting the people in your life is a gift of love to give.

The importance of personal connection is critical for all people to experience a fulfilling life. The feminine energy that resides within all of us has been powered over for centuries. We, as a collective, have incredible repair work to accomplish. The lessons I have gained through my study of the Seasons of the year also include immense work around the constructs of patriarchy. The power-over system that affects us all becomes more apparent when you witness this deconstruction in the people you love.

We have to connect back to ourselves to see and feel our power. This is how we begin to heal. When we feel our own power by connection to ourselves, our inner Maiden, Mother, and Crone, the Earth Mother and nature, that is how we will heal the collective. Unfortunately, the collective of men, women, children, animals, and our Earth continue to feel the pains of this power-over. And when you get to the point of seeing all the destruction, it can be incredibly overwhelming, lonely, and scary.

To overcome these sensations in your healing journey, you have to also connect with other women. This is also a key to experiencing a fulfilling life. In addition, it is how we heal ourselves and each other. Circle with women, sit knee-to-knee, and listen to each other. Be present with the other women's heartache, joys, celebrations, and devastations. We all have to witness each other in our growth and healing. This, in turn, gives women permission to grow and heal.

Reach out to your community of women, and if you need circle work and support, there are so many beautiful places to find these circles. Here are some places to start:

- Local yoga studios
- Non-denominational churches, or Unitarian Churches
- The Wild Women Project (www.wildwomenproject.com)
- Mother's groups
- Local New Age or Spiritual shops
- Spiritual Centers

When you feel into your power, you heal the constructs of power-over that have plagued our cultures for generations. I have trust in a system of healing ancestral pains. Do the work for yourself, do it for your daughter, do it for the Maidens who are finding themselves, do it for your Mother, her Mother, and her Mother. Do the work of healing so our world can feel more peace and love. It is that simple.

DESIRE FOR WOMEN TO FOLLOW THEIR PATH

I hope that my journey out of a marriage and into myself provides nuggets of inspiration. Whether you are on a similar path or a completely different journey, we are all experiencing a human life together. We can all continue to live in the constructs of our societal norms and check all the boxes of the life lists, or we can fit into the constructs of "boxes" themselves.

I realize all I have endured in such a short, concise period. Forty-five years of life and a mere two years of deconstruction and reconstruction have yielded so many lessons learned along the way. My heart is so full of gratitude for seeing how my path veered based on societal constructs but was able to create a new route by foraging through the rough terrain.

I hope that my story provides awareness around the idea that you have full permission to change yourself at any point of your life, whether you are in the Season of Maiden, the Season of the Mother, or the Season of the Crone. So continue to connect with yourself and listen to your intuitive wisdom within. Reflect on your journey while staying present and open to your now.

Listen to your Maiden if you are in your forties, and listen to your Crone if you are living through your thirties. Our wisdom is there; our knowledge of who and what we are meant to be, meant to do, and how we are supposed to show up for ourselves is all inside your heart. Your heart is your compass. When we listen to our hearts, we honor our best lives and our best selves. You are the only person in your life who will be able to determine the look and feel of your happiness.

May the Maidens have permission to amble through life rather than rush through it, checking boxes as our society encourages.

May they have the ability to love and marry their Selves first.

May they experience the rush of adventure and exploration of their minds and hearts and the wilderness.

May the Mothers feel the warmth of the love they deserve in return.

May their hearts never be broken by those who can quickly turn their backs on their love, honesty, and trust.

May the Mothers love vibrate unconditionally and honor intense love for ourselves and each other daily.

May the Crone be revered by all that walk beside her.

May we all sit at her feet to hear her speak her wisdom and truly listen to all the stories she has to tell.

May the Crone hold reverence in our hearts for all she has endured in this life, the journeys of her past, and the lessons of her future life still to come.

Letter to My Reader, Present time

Dear Reader,

What a year it has been! Thank you for your love and support as you have journeyed with me through the Seasons of the year. You have followed me as I acknowledged my desired change in Autumn to the dismantling of my marriage in the cold, dark Winter months. You have seen the rebuilding of myself and my life as I sprouted courage and a new way of being in Spring. And then finally, the recreation of a new way of living and being in the heat of the Summer.

I am honored that you were able to hold the space for me as I shared openly and vulnerably this massive year of transformation. I am fully aware that each of us has our trials and tribulations in this life, and that we all have a story that should be recognized. We may all have a week, a month, or a year of a life-impacting transition, and I am grateful that you allowed me to share my story with you.

My hope, dear Reader, is if you have a story to tell, you have all the courage to share yours. May the tools I have shared in this book give you comfort as you face any challenging circumstances in your own life. Allow the Seasons of the year to bring connection for you to our natural world. Allow each Season of your life to bring you the lessons you need so that you may become the very best version of yourself.

Wishing you all the best in your Heart & Soul,

Kerry Hope

CONNECTING TO YOUR MOTHER WISDOM: VISUALIZATION

Before you read this next section, please find yourself in a place of peace and solitude. Have a journal and pen nearby (or use this book to jot down any notes) so that you may capture any wisdom you gain as you connect to your inner knowing from your inner Mother archetype.

Pause now to close your eyes, and take three slow, deep, long, rich breaths in and out.

As you settle into yourself, begin by noticing all your sensations around your body. What does your clothing feel like on your skin? Are you warm, or is there a chill in the air? What smells do you notice around you? How does this book feel in your hands or on your lap? Step yourself through all five senses of your being.

How, at this moment, are you caring for your personal needs? Then, adjust yourself accordingly, and provide any additional comforts for yourself. For example, are your toes covered with cozy socks or a blanket? Do your shoulders feel wrapped up and secure? Or do you need a gentle breeze of a fan to keep you cool?

You are being held with so much love right now. Notice how it feels in your body when you can remember a warm embrace. Notice how it feels in your body when you think of an arm wrapped around your shoulder and soft words of praise are spoken to you. When you receive a text from a friend who shares gratitude for all you do, these are the sensations of love. You deserve to feel welcomed, cared for, nurtured, and loved.

To honor the warmth in your heart and this beautiful day of sunshine, you decided to pack up a little picnic of your favorite indulgences. You create a small basket of goodies containing your favorite cheese, slices of apples and grapes, the gluten-free crackers you love, a handful of chocolate-covered almonds, and sparkling water. You grab a blanket and head out for the nearby grassy knoll to sit, read, enjoy the bird songs, and nibble on delicious treats.

You identify the perfect spot in the shade, lay out your blanket, then kick off your shoes before you plop down to initiate the sacred time alone. This is the perfect day. The slight breeze feels fantastic on your warm skin, and the clouds float effortlessly above the sky. Finally, you open your basket of foods and begin to pull out each item you lovingly packaged.

You hear a voice come up from behind you, *"Hello darling, care if I join you?"* You are taken back to see yourself as a Mother. If you are not yet in the Mother stage of life, this will be your future Self. If you reside in the Crone Season of your life, this is your younger Mother Self. Or, if you are in the Mother Season of your life, she is showing up to you now.

You notice her strength and beauty as she kicks off her shoes to join you on your blanket. She is smiling and seems eager to have your attention. *"Did you bring our favorite chocolate-covered almonds?"* She asks eagerly. You respond to her and offer her all you have set out to enjoy.

"I want you to know that in this Season of Life, you are strong and able to get through all that may be challenging you. We can endure and thrive in all the hardships that come our way. But, we cannot continue to give until we can learn to take care of our Selves first and foremost truly."

How do her words settle in your heart? What are the challenges that she may be referring to for you? For example, what comes to mind in how you can better "take care" of yourself?

As you process her message, she reaches over and grabs your hand to hold. *"I will always be here to protect you, and . . ."* What else does she want you to know at this time?

Listen carefully.

You look her in the eyes and see that she is pouring herself and her love into you. You may become overwhelmed with her compassion, and you both tear up in a loving expression.

You say, *"Mother, thank you for being here with me now. Thank you for all of the love and support you have given. I give so much daily to my* (Fill in any category: family, children, parents, pets, career, passion projects, house, garden, community). *Thank you for permitting me to give to myself too. It feels good to be acknowledged and appreciated."*

Mother nods knowingly, as she too gave and gave, and similar to you, wants to feel the love in return. What other words come to your heart that you can now share with your inner Mother?

Take a deep breath to feel the exchange of love, kindness, and compassion.

You embrace each other one last time, and as she starts to pick herself up off the blanket, she grabs one little chocolate-covered almond, pops it into her mouth, smiles, and gives you a wink. She stands up and gets her shoes back on her feet. As she begins to walk away, knowing the importance of your sacred time alone, she does one last turn around and says,

"I love you, always and forever."

You smile, reach for your journal and pen that you thankfully remembered to bring along, and begin writing down all the loving thoughts Mother shared with you. Any wisdom, advice, or just feelings and sensations you experienced during your time with her.

Write for the next few moments. Take time to write a letter to your Mother Self, your actual mother, or any woman who is a significant mother in your life.

V

SEASONAL WISDOM, RITUALS, AND ANCHORS

CLEAR TO CLEANSE RITUAL

We live in spaces that hold so much energy. Our society pressures us into unhealthy consumerism. Even if we are not guilty of buying unnecessary goods, I can assure you extra items, and things can pile up in the corners of your home.

All the stuff in our homes holds energy. In some cases, this energy can affect your daily energy too. You will find that your overall energy will shift once you implement these seasonal rituals. If you are able, find a few hours at the start of each Season for your Clear to Cleanse Ritual.

Keeping the space in which you reside healthy and clean will, in fact, keep your vibrations of energy higher in your environment too.

Turn on your favorite upbeat playlist and room by room, go through your home and reduce the clutter holding unnecessary energy.

- Storage Clutter: Drawers in kitchen, linen, hallway closets, bedroom closets, bathroom vanity/cabinetry.

- Obvious Clutter: Items left out on tables, other surfaces, or items piled on floors.

Box, label, or store (in one location if possible) previous Season items that float around your house. These include:

- Autumn: Summer beach or pool gear, flip-flops, sandals, sun hats, sports gear, etc.

- Winter: Fall coats, shoes, sports gear, holiday decor, and Halloween costumes too.

- Spring: Winter coats, boots, scarves, hats, gloves, holiday decor.

- Summer: Spring coats, boots, Spring activity gear, etc.

Go through all seasonal clothing for yourself and with your housemates.

- What is still in good condition that could be passed along to others?

- Create piles for donations or to pass along to friends or their children.

- Place clothing items you intend to keep and wear next year into a container or rotate them to the back section of your closet. Repeat this process for shoes. This one is always tough for me.

Go through Refrigerator/Freezer/Pantry

- What are expired or unhealthy items you no longer need?
- Can any non-perishable items be donated to the local food pantry?

Repeat the cleaning process for each room in your home, and set a timer for each room so that you don't go down a huge rabbit hole each Season. Keep moving through the process so that it doesn't overwhelm you. Ask family and friends to help.

Keep only the sacred items, and focus on non-attachment as you go. If you don't have a deep connection to an object, ask yourself why you are holding on to it. Honor your answers, but also be prepared to let go. This process keeps the flow of abundance in your life. Keeping your space cleared signals to the universe that you are open to receiving: more love, more wisdom, more health, more financial abundance, more happiness, more of whatever your heart desires for the Season

AUTUMN SEASON: MOTHER AND CRONE WISDOM

Your Mother and Crone archetypes are always here to support you. Your inner Mother and inner Crone energy allow you to create an existence where you can honor yourself and the Seasons of your life. You can incorporate one or several of these practices into your routine during your Autumn Season.

Autumn Altar Space Creation

At the beginning of the Autumn Season, find a little space in your living environment designated just for you. I realize this can be a challenge sometimes, and I also hear that cats completely ignore this boundary.

Ideas of a space designated just for you might include:

- A corner in a large room for a yoga mat and pillows.
- A mantle or hearth of a fireplace.
- A desk or table used for creating (preferably not a workspace).
- A dresser or shelf in a bedroom.
- An available unused closet space (bravo to those that have this!).
- A window sill or space in the kitchen that would not be disturbed day-to-day.

Get creative. If finding a space is a challenge, ask your space mates, family, and friends to help you brainstorm a solution. This unique sacred space is where I encourage you to create your Seasonal Altar.

Place a candle on your altar, but only light it when you dedicate yourself to the space. Please use it safely.

Many people like to use different types of smoke to clear their space. Smoke Rituals are powerful and have been used by many Indigenous people and cultures for thousands of years. Sage is the most common plant that people know to use for smoke clearing. However, you can also use palo santo sticks, sweet grass, dried herbs and flowers, and any type of incense you love.

Autumn Equinox: Gratitude Jar Ritual

The Autumn Equinox takes place around September 21st each year. Around this time of the year, take a walk in a nearby park or around your yard. Notice all the types of leaves, ornamental grasses, sticks, rocks, and nuts (acorns from trees are especially magical).

Intentionally choose and collect a few items, holding our Mother Earth in your heart. Ask her for permission to take the sacred objects, and of course, thank her as you go. Bring these items back to your altar space, clean the area, and clear it by removing dust and clutter.

You can initiate your Gratitude Ritual with a smoke clearing, or cleanse your altar space energy with music, drumming, a rattle, or even clapping the area clear with your own hands. Get creative, and speak an intention into this process from your heart. For example, "I am freeing all the unwanted energy from this space, opening up for fresh, new energy to enter."

Place a large glass vase, jar, or container in the center of your altar space. Bonus points if the jar can receive natural sunlight during the day.

Next, write down what you are grateful for in this Season on small pieces of paper. Some examples could include: people, pets, friends, career, endeavors, clean water, and nourishing foods.

List anything and everything that comes to your heart in this creative moment. Fill your jar with the sentiments of gratitude you hold in your heart. Continue to add each day through the Season.

Then, place any additional items on the altar to support your gratitude—a candle, a figurine or piece of art, or a photo that promotes your Autumn abundance.

Give each item a welcome to the altar space with a blessing or a simple "Thank you."

Next, bring in the items from your nature walk and decorate your altar. As you place each item, give it an intention: "With this leaf, I intend to let go of what is no longer serving my highest good." Or, "May this rock represent the grounding earth energy I need to keep me solid in my dedication to eating healthy this Season."

Once you have all items set in the way that pleases your Soul, ask your higher Self if it feels complete. If you feel a visceral "Yes," you can close your altar creation session.

Light a candle, journal your intentions for the Season. Then, put on your favorite playlist and dance. Or continue to sit quietly with your altar and listen.

Your Autumn Altar Ritual can be undone at the end of the Autumn Season or before Winter Solstice. Working in reverse, thank each item for its support, protection, or holding an intention with you, disassemble the additional items mindfully. The gratitude jar can be emptied. You can alchemize your gratitude by burning the paper into the ether and speaking aloud, "All that I am grateful for and even more, continues to grow. Thank you, and so it is."

All nature items can go back out to the earth, thanking our Mother, Gaia, or Poncahmama (all the archetypes of the Goddesses representing Mother Earth).

Anchors for Autumn Season

Slow Down

- Start to notice how you walk in and out of the parking lot to the grocery store. Intentionally slow your steps.
- Can you slow down your pace when walking during the day, around your home, your work, and to and from all places?
- We need to signal to your bodies that we are getting ready for rest.
- We can release the fire and Summer energy and slow our roll.
- Slow down how you prepare and eat your meals.
- Say "no" to optional or new events and activities. This creates more space around what you are already obligated to do or attend.
- When you find slowness in your steps and breath, you can repeat the Mantra in your mind or aloud: "I am Divinely Connected to my inner wisdom and love." Or "I am fully present in my moment and my heart."

Ground Your Self

The shifts between Seasons can be overwhelming if you are not grounding yourself. We can instantly feel more grounded when we have direct contact and connection to Mother Earth.

- Take advantage of the last warm days to walk barefoot in your yard or on the grass at the park.
- Start establishing a new routine and creating a new Autumn Ritual for grounding. Examples could be a hot Epsom salt bath (not as popular in the hot Summer months) or a warm tea at the end of the day.

Protect Your Body

The transition into cooler temperatures in the Autumn Season should not be shocking to your system. Be prepared and support your body.

- Start to gather all the items that physically keep your body warm and cozy.
- Dry clean or launder your favorite Winter coats and sweaters.
- Clean off the dirt from your boots or shoes.

- Fill a tote or basket with your favorite fall scarves and hats to have them available when you venture outside in the cooler weather.

Eat Warm Foods

For me, Autumn is the SOUP season. So many beautiful recipes for fall harvest-inspired foods.

Create an Autumn Season shopping list and stock your fridge and pantry with essential ingredients to nourish your body.

- Start to incorporate more meals with warm, moist foods.
- Pears are the perfect fruit for your body in the fall.
- Body Oil Ritual
- Create a daily body oil practice after you shower or take a hot bath in the evening.
- Slow down and take your time as you lather your body with sesame, coconut, or body oil. These oils will keep your skin healthy and protected.
- Mix in geranium, lavender, and ylang-ylang essential oils for an extra Autumn Season experience.
- A mantra to repeat in your body oil ritual could be, "I am fully in my body. I am expressive, and speak my truth daily."

WINTER SEASON: CRONE WISDOM

Your Crone is excited to have your attention this Winter Season. It is the Season of Rest and Regeneration. As you continue on your journey through the Seasons, you have an opportunity to learn how to embrace the sweetness of Winter. Crone energy asks you to use your inner wisdom, honor your boundaries, and take great care of your body. Here are ways to create rituals and practices for your Winter Season.

Winter Altar Space Creation

At the beginning of the Winter Season, find a little space in your living environment designated just for you. Winter Solstices occur on or around December 21 each year. Your Winter Solstice altar can also bring in any other holiday decor that brings you joy. For example, you can utilize your altar space to include the lighting of a Menorah or add seven items to represent the principles of Kwanzaa.

This space can be a place for you to rest this Season, or it can be a place that you can visually see while you are resting. If you have warmth in Winter Season, there could be options for an outside altar. Looking through your space, find a place just for you that will not be compromised for the Season.

Begin by clearing the energy of your space.

Using smoke to clear (see Autumn Altar Space Creation), or using sound with a rattle, a drum, or clapping your hands. Also, you can speak an affirmation into the space, "I intend to create an altar to honor:

- Winter Solstice - The shortest day of the year."
- My Crone Energy."
- My Cozy Heart."
- My Ancestors."
- Or anything specific to your religious practices this time of year.
- Speak: "I am asking for all unwanted energies to now leave this space."

Establish a theme for your altar, then set one main object to represent your Winter Altar:

- A beautiful candle for warmth.
- An evergreen wreath for eternal life.
- A photo of yourself (if you are in the Season of Crone) or your Mother, Grandmother, or any person who has guided you.
- Pine cones, dried leaves, or any other dried grasses you can find outside on a park walk or in your yard are perfect ways to honor the dormant Season.

Be cautious as you choose and place your items on the altar. Make sure all candle flames are safe from other objects. Once you have created the perfect altar for your Soul and your space, finish up with a beautiful message of gratitude, or close your eyes and speak a blessing from your heart.

Winter Solstice: Witches Ball Ritual

A Witches Ball can be created in Winter and best around the Solstice. They can correlate with the holiday tradition of tree ornaments but are not significant to any holiday. As a 17th Century tradition brought to the United States from England, these decorative ornaments were used to ward off evil spirits, illness, and bad fortune and energies. More so, they protect the space in which they are hung. These can stay up all year. However, the Crone wisdom would encourage you to release all the energy they catch and create a new Witches Ball each Winter Solstice. Create a witches ball alone or with some of your closest friends as you cozy in for a beautiful Winter gathering. Here are the steps:

You will need a clear glass ball ornament with an opening on the top or side, wide enough to allow your fingers in to create.

- Make a base with either dried herbs or mosses, adding all of these or some: Cinnamon sticks to bring in good fortune. Sage leaves and stems for protection. Lavender for soothing. Add either a piece of black tourmaline or labradorite for protective energies.

- Add a shiny thread (gold or silver) that can be tied into an infinity knot or a figure 8 shape. The shiny thread attracts the negative energy and locks it up like an entangled web.

- You can add any additional trinkets or items that support your intentions of protection. You are the creative genius here!

- You can also paint your ball if you like. Allow your inner Crone to lead you.

- Tie a string to hang your Witches Ball and give it a little blessing. Hang it in an EAST facing window in your home, office space, or wherever you feel you need protection.

While making your ornament, be conscious of your intentions for this art that will support you and protect you for the coming Season and Year ahead. Your Winter Solstice Ritual is complete.

Anchors for Winter Season

Honoring Rest & Restoration

The Season of Rest! Winter is our time.

- Say "no" to any unnecessary events or commitments.
- Say "thank you" to all that we have accomplished this year.
- Honor the moments to be still.
- Give attention to the stack of books on the nightstand as you crawl into your bed a little earlier each night.
- Sit next to your home altar, fireplace, or favorite candle and sip a hot tea.
- Find a cozy corner for a gentle stretch or restorative yoga postures in your home.

Hydrate with Warm Water

- Lemon and honey, ginger, and mint are great additional ways to sip your way to hydration.
- Having all the ingredients ready to go next to your tea kettle or water heater makes this routine easier to accomplish when you wake in the morning.
- Sipping warm lemon water in the evening is also very beneficial.

Journaling Practice

- Since the Winter days have fewer daylight hours, this is the perfect Season to write and reflect.
- Invest in a journal or notepad that you love to see and hold and a pen that allows your thoughts to flow.
- This is an excellent Season to reflect on all you have learned from the previous three Seasons in the calendar year.
- It is also an excellent time to look forward to new intentions, ideas, and accomplishments you would like to obtain for the next three Seasons ahead.

Get Outside

- Don't let the cooler temperatures keep you homebound.

- Protect your skin with warm layers. It is vital to continue to connect with nature and allow the crisp air to reach your lungs.

- Enjoy the time with a friend to hold each other accountable.

Honoring Pleasure

Indulge in and give attention to all your senses this Season!

Enjoy the luxurious hot baths with essential oils that bring your senses alive. Suggested oils to use in body ritual: cinnamon, clove, orange, sandalwood, peppermint, ginger.

- Wear all the soft and comfy clothing that cuddles you up.

- While cozy in your own home, wear the sexy lingerie that makes you feel empowered.

- Lathering your body with oils and lotions to keep your skin protected can also be a way to love yourself!

- Indulge in sweet, mouthwatering treats, and enjoy all the pleasures that may come from your music or the sounds of a crackling fire.

SPRING SEASON: MAIDEN WISDOM

The Maiden is alive, energetic, and enthusiastic. This is the Season of new beginnings, play, and creative expression. Stretch yourself awake and allow the budding and renewal that Mother Earth provides as your playground for enjoyment and fun. The Maiden encourages you to embrace the Season of Spring with open arms and an open heart. Here are the ways to bring Spring Season to life.

Spring Altar Space Creation

The Spring Altar Creation practice can be a new, different space from the Autumn and Winter Altar, or it can be the same space but altered. The Spring altar can be set up outside, on a front porch, or in a garden, depending on your climate.

Once you have your designated space, clear or clean all objects if any exist.

- Diffuse essential oils, or create a room spray of half distilled water mixed with an essential oil perfect for Spring. (Some ideas: rosemary, frankincense, tangerine, spearmint, or Roman chamomile.) The essential oils (or blend of e.o.) will set the clearing intention for your altar.

- Start by laying down a scarf for a tapestry full of color – bright and cheery – as a base on your surface.

- Then, blessing each personal item one at a time, set an intention to what that item will bring in for your this Spring Season.

- Examples: fresh flowers for growth, seeds you intend to plant, bunny statues for energy, eggs (dye with natural colors, or confetti eggs) for fertility.

- A photo of you as a Maiden. Place a recent photo of you being expressive and playful if you are currently in the Maiden Season of Life.

- Any additional items that bring joy, love, and a smile to your face.

Thank your Maiden archetype for showing up to create a beautiful space and a reminder for you to enjoy this Season of Spring.

Spring Equinox: Maiden Flower Crown Ritual

The Spring Equinox occurs around March 21 every year. Now is when we shake off our Winter energy and bring more light, playful fun into our lives. The Season to honor our Maiden can be so uplifting and energizing. A favorite ritual of mine is to create a flower crown to honor the youthful beauty that you still carry throughout all your Seasons.

Creating art is a beautiful way to bring out the Maiden, but I have found a key element to crafting is my Maiden playlist. Use a streaming music app to create this playlist, or write down all of your favorite songs from your youthful teenage years and create one on your own. The nostalgia of this music will be a perfect muse.

If you are similar to me, looking for a pair of scissors in the middle of a project can lead to emptying a dishwasher. So, Make sure you have all your supplies and materials ready before you begin this crafting project.

A Maiden Flower Crown can be as simple as tying together dandelions to create a circle to wear at the crown of your head. This activity can be very therapeutic when you combine it with a Spring picnic in a field of dandelions. (Make sure to thank the bees!) However, I have crafted Maiden Flower Crowns multiple times with women, many of whom have created incredible and intricate masterpieces to be adorned on their heads. The bigger, the better rule can apply to Maiden Flower Crowns, and the sweetest, most simple headpieces can be equally stunning.

Starting with the Crown base, you can measure the diameter of your head and use this measurement to create a base in which to build. You can use a flexible wire, a pipe cleaner, or keep it all-natural with thin branches or long twigs that can easily bend and tie into a circle.

Once you have a base for your crown, the options are truly endless for how you adorn this crown to meet your aesthetic or empowerment needs. Use lots of flowers (dried, real, or silk), ribbon, yarn, dried grasses, herbs, leaves, tree bark, dried moss, sparkly glitter, stones, tiny crystals, or jewelry.

This is your crown, so finding ways to incorporate your intentions behind the flower crown is beneficial to the ritual. Feel free to keep trying it on throughout the process (having a mirror around is helpful) and ask: *What else does my Maiden want to wear on this crown?*

Once your Spring Equinox Maiden Flower Crown is complete, finish the ritual with a good clean-up and tidy session of your crafting area. Make sure you turn up your favorite Maiden Playlist song for this! Then, wearing this Maiden Flower Crown, a dance session to honor your inner Maiden energy is essential. This can be done in the privacy of your own space, or including other women in this ritual makes it even juicier.

Once you feel complete with your ritual. Be sure to thank your Maiden Self for showing up to play. You can set your Maiden Flower Crown on your Spring Altar as a reminder to be playful, sensual, and whatever your Spring Equinox intentions are for the Season. Once you move into Summer Equinox, you can disassemble the crown, ensuring that all the natural items are released back to the earth for composting.

Thank you, Gaia. Thank you, Maiden. And so it shall be!

Anchors for Spring Season

Move Your Body and Dance

- Put on your favorite genre of music or your favorite artist when you were a pre-teen/teenager and just dance around.

- Move your body. Move your feet, legs, belly, hips, and arms.

- Dance around your kitchen while prepping food or in the privacy of your bathroom as you get ready for the day.

- There are so many ways you can incorporate a fun way to release your inner Maiden. When you move your body, you will be surprised at the lightness and love that will flood into you.

PLAY!

Spring is the Season of play and for many of us, getting outside allows us to feel these sensations calling.

- Riding bikes, walking in the park, or even swinging on the swing set at the park.

- Notice how you feel when you allow yourself to laugh and be silly.

- The surge of energy we feel when we allow ourselves to play and be free can be transferred and reverberated to all those around us.

Create Something, Create Anything

Spring is the perfect time to create an art piece for your home, garden, something you can wear or give to a friend. Making art can be anything: music, paintings, jewelry, a scrapbook.

- Get outside and create a Mandala or art design using twigs, rocks, pine cones, flowers, and weeds. It's okay if you spend just a few moments of your time creating a little something that allows freedom of expression.

- Create a new altar for Spring to celebrate a Goddess, a deity, or even your favorite character in a book.
- See what your creative genius is capable of making. The most important thing is not judging your art or how it looks. Whatever you create is one-of-a-kind, and there will never be a replica of your creation.

Express Yourself!

- What would your inner Maiden like for you to wear to a dinner with friends? Dig out that beautiful scarf you have been waiting to wear, or try that cute new braid you saw on social media.
- Try a different eye shadow color combination of the untouched colors that sit patiently waiting in your eye-color pallet.
- Spring is a great time to wear bright, bold colors, floral prints, and cute hats.
- Stepping outside of your comfort zone can be incredibly empowering.

Earthing/Grounding Walks

This is an essential practice all year round. The Spring Season is different when you can get your feet on the ground or earth, especially for those who have cold climate Winters.

- Getting barefoot and dancing, playing, expressing yourself, creating art, all the other anchors can be magnified when you allow for bare feet.
- Mantras to speak while going on a grounding meditation walk:

"I am Conscious."

"I am Empowered."

"I am a beautiful Creative Expression."

SUMMER SEASON: MOTHER WISDOM

The Mother archetype is here to support you in this bountiful Season. The Mother as planet Earth, shares her fullest of gifts with all the natural life in bloom. When you find more moments in Summer to be present with the natural world, you will be able to be more present with yourself. To demonstrate the beauty of Mother energy, be generous with your love and compassion to all the beings, plants, and animals. Oh, and your Mother asks for you to clean up your room.

Summer Altar Space Creation

The Summer Solstice takes place on or around June 21 each year and is a perfect time to create your Summer Altar space. If the opportunity allows you to have a little room to create an altar outside, which feels good to you, then do so! Once you have your designated area, clear or clean all objects if any exist.

- Clear the space with either a smoke clearing ritual or a sound clearing with a rattle, drum, clapping your hands, or speaking an intentional message to remove unwanted energy.

- Place a cloth, a table placemat, or a base such as a tray in your desired spot.

- Summer is a great time of year to add gifts from Mother Earth to honor her. If you walk around in a park, natural setting, or even in your yard, ask for permission to take any flowers, sticks, rocks, downed limbs or branches, etc. It's just the right thing to do.

- Once you've collected all your goodies for the altar, thank Mother Earth and give her a blessing in exchange. Or, leave a little treasure at the base of a tree, such as a small earring that has lost its mate. You also can sprinkle corn starch at the bottom of a tree with a message of gratitude for all that she provides.

- Create a theme for your altar, or dedicate the altar to your Mother archetype, your very own mother, or Mother Earth.

- Place a photo of yourself on the altar if you are in the Season of the Mother, or a photo of a mother for whom you love and care.

- Add each item one at a time, setting the intention for what each object represents for this Summer Season.

- Flowers represent my ability to bloom and grow, or the individual beauty in all of us.

- Bird feathers (if you find one, look up the bird for animal totem meaning!) could represent your freedom to be your own individual Self.

- Add anything that might represent nurturing to you (body oils can infuse energy).

- Little figurines special to you (perhaps you received something like this as a gift from your mother).

- A candle to remind you to keep shining your light.

Once you feel your altar is complete and all your intentions for the Summer Season have been set, you can close your altar ritual with a statement from your heart. This is your space to come back to anytime to reflect or keep adding other treasures that you might find.

Summer Solstice: Mother Prayer Tree Ritual

Summer Solstice is the initiation of the Summer Season on or around June 21. On this day, we celebrate the longest day of the year, with the most amount of sunlight exposure, giving brightness and power to support our Mother Season. This is the time of year when we can feel into the fullness of our passions and power. Embracing all of our capabilities to give big love and feel into that energy.

Regardless of where you are in your Seasons of Life, you can always tap into the power of protection and prayer that comes naturally to the Mother archetype. This is the time to honor Mother Earth, including all human and animal creatures who live with her protection and blessing.

The Mother Prayer Tree Ritual can be completed in one time frame and setting or can be carried out through the length of the Summer. If you have a particular tree that you love and is accessible where you live, start there. Suppose you don't have a favorite tree. In that case, there are multiple ways you can create this ritual by simply going to a nearby park, visiting a shrub near your home, or even using a house plant.

To begin, collect scrap pieces of cloth or ribbons. If you don't have any scraps or ribbons on hand, cut up an old dishrag or t-shirt. Place the items in a basket to carry to your 'tree.' Once you have your basket filled with offerings, give the basket a verbal blessing or clear it with smoke or sound to eliminate any unwanted energy.

When you find the moment to create your Mother Prayer Tree Ritual, allow yourself plenty of time and limited distractions. This ritual can be completed with family and friends or alone.

Taking in three deep cleansing breaths, begin your ritual with a statement of intention for the Summer Season: "In this Season of Summer, I will honor the love that the great Mother demonstrates to me each day. I will be mindful of all the ways I can give my love and support my passions and the passions of those around me."

This is just an example. Create the Summer intention that feels best for you.

Picking one piece of material up at a time, close your eyes and say a prayer representing that particular scrap or ribbon. Then, tie the ribbon onto a tree branch (shrub, plant, etc.). You will repeat this process until all of your materials are infused with a prayer or intention.

Pray for all the people in your life or those you may not know but could use prayer and support. Say a prayer for your own animals and the animals that need prayer and support. Say a prayer for the miracles you are allowing to come to you now. Say a prayer for those on our planet who might need a miracle right now. Think of everyone and everything that comes to your heart in this moment of ritual.

Be creative and sincere. Once all the pieces of material are tied to your tree, you can now say a final statement of completion. "Great Mother, please hold each of these prayers, with your immense amount of love and protection in this Season. We are forever grateful for your love."

If anything else needs to be said or spoken, feel free to add to your ritual. Bring a blanket and favorite snacks to the tree throughout the Summer and sit with your Mother. As the Season ends, remove each tied piece of material and return words of gratitude for each prayer.

Anchors for Summer Season

Soak in the Sun

- Hats and long-sleeves keep the dangerous sun rays away, but you still can soak in the energy of the sun, the warmth, and heat—the vibes of all the plants and animals that are thriving in this Season.

- Don't forget your SPF (Reef friendly for our beachfront gals).

Body Transportation Station

- Move your body and make tracks. Walk, hike, bike, and run! Get outside to connect with your surroundings and your community.

- Finding transportation body movement creates new perspectives and insights along the route.

- Road trips in Summer can also be incredibly healing.

Eat Fresh, Cooling Foods

- Garden fresh veggies are in abundance this Season.

- Head to your local farmer's market on the weekends, or exchange an hour of weeding for veggies from friends and family who have a garden.

- Cucumbers, melons, coconut, bananas, and berries are excellent to add to your meals or snacks. They are a great way to help regulate your body in the heat. Green, bitter-flavored veggies are the best to consume.

Embrace the Element of Water

Water yourself every Season, but make it grand in the Summer heat.

- Hydrate your body! Drinking recommended daily amounts of water for your body is essential.

- Ensure you are also getting enough electrolytes and the twelve essential salts to regulate your body.

- Don't forget to splash in creeks, rivers, and lakes! Safely swim in ponds, oceans, rivers, and pools. Allow yourself time to play. You can even create a fountain with your back patio hose!

Mother Yourself

This is the Season of the Mother.

- Find ways to love up on yourself with sweet treats.
- Enjoy the longer days by swinging in a hammock or creating loving travel memories for yourself.
- Spray yourself with Rosewater (half distilled water and a few drops of rose essential oil; lavender and spearmint also work great).
- Wrap your arms around yourself every day and say three things you love about yourself. Body, Mind, and Spirit are three categories on which to focus.
- Love yourself up with positive messages or mantras:

    "I am love. I am Loved. I Love."

    "I am a nurturing Soul that loves to connect with people in my life who love me as I am."

    "In Summer, I am full of life, and expression of life comes easefully for me."

EPILOGUE

In the 2020 health pandemic, people worldwide experienced significant losses. Losing family members and friends to the COVID-19 virus was devastating to so many. Even those fortunate folks who were able to stay healthy experienced consequential loss too. Loss of jobs, homes, and dreams. The loss of experiences from high school graduations to weddings and many other forsaken moments of celebration. People lost their sense of community and human connection, which is detrimental in so many ways to the human psyche. Everyone experienced loss in some form, and we are collectively going through the stages of grief during this pandemic era.

I believe the pain of grief is a gift, though. I gained the heart's most incredible skills and lessons through all the pain and suffering I endured through the Seasons of my transition. I gained strength and confidence. I gained compassion and heart expansion. I was able to walk away with treasures I wasn't expecting: forgiveness, perspective, and acceptance of others' life experiences. The biggest treasure I found during this challenging and complex time, though, is Self-Love.

I loved and nurtured myself through grief and learned how to manage the rollercoaster ride of emotions of the process. I also knew that the suffering wasn't always mine. I was grieving the sadness and loss of close friends and the collective of all humans experiencing a significant loss. I realized that I had unprocessed grief from other losses, such as losing a father to cancer, a miscarriage, and a sense of identity.

At the end of the rollercoaster ride of grief, I genuinely saw that love was the reason behind it all. It all comes back to love. In reflection, I can see the pain and grief I experienced after losing love for a husband for so many years. I can witness the mystery behind the unforeseen loss of my beautiful sense of Self and the closeness of my relationships with my mother and some of my best friends. All of this pain and loss led to grief. However, on the other side of this grief was my greater ability to love: to love the people in my life, past and present, and then to recognize and see that I had unconditional love for myself.

Loving myself first—respecting myself and knowing what is for my highest good in this life, has been a radical act of Self-Love. And from it, the right relationships have shown up for me, and those relationships that were not for my highest good have fallen away. I stayed dedicated to my health and emotional well-being, which turned out to be such a gift.

May we all learn from our experiences in our lives and find the hidden golden treasures and shimmery gifts that the Seasons present to us. As we continue to traverse our paths in this life together, let us see each other's lights shining through each Season of the Year. May we always know we are not alone as we traverse through the Seasons of our Lives. Your inner knowing and wisdom will always carry you to a greater version of yourself.

Looking forward,

Kerry Hope

FORESHADOW OF THE PONCHA MAMA TRAIL

In this moment, she felt so whole and complete that her world was at her feet, bowing down to the greatness of her heart and all that she accomplished in her life.

She knew she had more places to go and felt nothing would ever stop her. For once, she was sure that the love she gave would always come back to her from the love of the earth. The whispers of the trees and pink sky sunsets will continue to remind her of this love.

The story continued, the very moment that she met and fell in love with the woman who carries her heart each lifetime together. This moment was like no other, and she found herself surrounded by the creation and craft of all her visions that came to fruition.

The energy nearly took her breath away. She gazed at each of those with her, with love and gratitude in her eyes, and she smiled sweetly.

Only weeks before, she had been on the mountain with her community of wild women and knew that all her lessons, work, releases, shadows, and fears took a bow to her greatness.

She heard the trees remind her once again, "Stay Resilient," as they kissed her skin with the breeze.

It was there that the Great Provider truly found her ultimate gift to give upon her return.

Now, she knew what it meant to be wild and free. To embody this without additional guilt and shame brought her relief and acceptance. She relished in all that she had become and all that she was able to provide.

There was such profound joy in crafting her life and taking the time to reflect on her path and journey throughout each Season.

At this moment, if there is one thing she knows, it is this . . . The love she gives always comes back to her in even bigger and better greatness only because she fills her heart and Soul with gratitude every day.

Written by Kerry Hope

August 24, 2018

Wild Woman Fest Workshop

RESOURCES

What I Read and Heard to Support My Journey

BOOKS

- *Untamed* by Glennon Doyle
- *Keep Moving: Notes on Loss, Creativity, and Change* by Maggie Smith
- *40 Weeks: A Daily Journey of Inspiration and Abundance* by Heather Doyle Fraser
- *Nature and the Human Soul: Cultivating Wholeness and Community in a Fragmented World* by Bill Plotkins
- *Soul Craft: Crossing into the Mysteries of Nature and Psyche* by Bill Plotkin
- *Sacred Contracts: Awakening Your Divine Potential* by Caroline Myss
- *Nonviolent Communication: A Language of Life: Lifechanging Tools for Healthy Relationships* by Marshall Rosenberg
- *The Holy Wild: A Heathen Bible for the Untamed Women* by Danielle Dulsky
- *Braving The Wilderness: The Quest for True Belonging and the Courage to Stand Alone* by Brene Brown
- *When Things Fall Apart: Heart Advice for Difficult Times* by Pema Chodron
- *The Yamas & Niyamas: Exploring Yoga's Ethical Practice* by Deborah Adele
- *Heart Minded: How to Hold Yourself and Others in Love* by Sarah Blondin

- *Set Boundaries, Find Peace: A Guide to Reclaiming Yourself* by Nedra Glover Tawwab
- *The Book of Relief: Passages and Exercises to Relieve Negative Emotions and Create More East in The Body* by Emily Maroutian
- *Chakra Healing: A Beginner's Guide to Self Healing Techniques that Balance the Chakras* by Margarita Alcantara

Podcasts

- *The goop* ~ Gwyneth Paltrow
- *Unlocking Us* ~ Brene Brown
- *We Can Do Hard Things* ~ Glennon Doyle
- *With Love, Danielle* ~ Danielle LaPorte

Insight Timer Teachers

- Carrie Grossman
- Liza Colpa
- Sarah Blondin
- Tara Brach

Social Media & Influencers

- Austin Channing @austinchanning
- Awakened Goddess @awakened_goddesses
- Brene Brown @brenebrown
- Chani Nicholas @chaninicholas
- Danielle Dulsky @wolfwomanwitch
- Danielle LaPorte @daniellelaporte
- Dawn of the New Era @dawn_of_the_new_era

- Emily Nagoski @enagoski
- Glennon Doyle @glennondoyle
- House of AUM @houseofaumyoga
- Jane International @janeinternational
- Jasmine Grace @Iamjasminegrace
- Narcissistic Abuse Recovery @narc_proof_and_thriving
- Prentis Hemphill @prentishemphill
- Rewilding For Women @rewildingforwomen
- Rising Women @risingwoman
- Sarah Blondin @sarahfinds
- Sarah Durham Wilson @sarahofmagdalene
- Sister Cody@sistercody
- The Holistic Psychologist @the.holistic.psychologist
- The Moon Tarot @themoontarot
- The Wild Sage Collective @thewildsagecollective
- The Wild Woman Project @thewildwomanproject
- Yung Pueblo @yung_pueblo

ACKNOWLEDGMENTS

The people who come in and out of your life will always bring you gifts of learning. It is then up to you to see the value of those gifts. Heather Doyle Fraser came into my life Fall of 2014, and I had no idea the number of treasures I would gain from her for the next eight years of my life. The book, *Your Triple Goddess: A Path to Self-Love, Empowerment, and Healing* will be one of the greatest. Thank you, Heather, for holding my hand and heart through this writing process. You are such a gift to me.

My heart is filled with gratitude for my pack of wolf women. Each of you has played a significant supporting role in my story, and many of you are mentioned along the way. Upon waking every morning, I can feel each of your hands on my back through my journey. I will forever be in debt to all the love and support.

I will never be able to speak enough words of gratitude for Kristen Michelle. Thank you for standing by my side as we walk through the fire together. The view from the mountain top is pretty spectacular. I love you in all ways, for always.

Finally, to my greatest gifts in this life, my children. You are the reason for my bravery. I am honored to be your mother and grateful to experience unconditional love for you both.

ABOUT THE AUTHOR

Kerry Hope (She/Her) creates healing workshops and retreats which allow participants to embody connection to Self, Nature, and Community. She is the founder of *Sacred GEO Experiences*, a Circle Leader through *The Wild Woman Project*, and facilitates Women's Councils.

Kerry leads and holds space for women to be open and authentic and process emotions in supportive, safe environments. Through her Women's Councils, Kerry provides techniques and rituals for living healthy, connected lives within the Seasons of the year and utilizes creativity for healing expression.

Kerry creates an energetic, compassionate, and heart-centered space for everyone she encounters. Greeting each new day and person with optimism that she believes is the medicine for healing our world. She lives along the rural edges of the Geographical Center of Ohio with her two children, her partner, and three dogs.

Made in the USA
Columbia, SC
13 January 2023

10237129R00102